Cocktails &
fingerfood

Cocktails & fingerfood

Contents

Nibbles
& Starters

Fried whitebait

500 g (1 lb 2 oz) whitebait
2 teaspoons sea salt
2 tablespoons plain
   (all-purpose) flour
1½ tablespoons cornflour
   (cornstarch)
2 teaspoons finely chopped flat-leaf
   (Italian) parsley
vegetable oil, for deep-frying
lemon wedges, for serving

Combine the whitebait and sea salt in a bowl and mix well. Cover and refrigerate until needed.

Combine the sifted flours and parsley in a bowl and season well with freshly ground black pepper. Fill a deep-fat fryer or large saucepan one-third full of oil and heat to 180°C (350°F), or until a cube of white bread dropped into the oil browns in 15 seconds. Toss a third of the whitebait in the flour mixture, shake off the excess flour, and deep-fry for 1½ minutes, or until pale and crisp. Drain well on crumpled paper towels. Repeat with the remaining whitebait.

Just before serving, reheat the oil to 190°C (375°C), or until a cube of white bread browns in 10 seconds, and fry the whitebait a second time, in batches, for 1 minute each batch, or until lightly browned. Drain on crumpled paper towels, salt lightly (this will help absorb any excess oil) and serve while hot with some lemon wedges.

Serves 4

Crunchy wedges

6 floury or all-purpose potatoes
1 tablespoon oil
25 g (¼ cup) dry breadcrumbs
2 teaspoons chopped chives
1 teaspoon celery salt
¼ teaspoon garlic powder
½ teaspoon chopped rosemary

Preheat the oven to 200°C (400°F/ Gas 6). Cut the potatoes into eight wedges each and toss in the oil.

Combine the breadcrumbs, chives, celery salt, garlic powder and rosemary in a bowl. Add the wedges and coat well. Place on greased baking trays and bake for 40 minutes, or until crisp and golden.

Makes 48

Deep-fried cheese ravioli

oil, for deep-frying
300 g (10½ oz) fresh cheese ravioli
  (see Notes)

Fill a deep heavy-based saucepan or deep-fryer one-third full of oil and heat to 180°C (350°F), or until a cube of bread dropped into the oil browns in 15 seconds. Cook the ravioli in batches until golden brown.

Remove from the oil and drain on crumpled paper towels. Sprinkle with salt and cracked black pepper, and serve hot.

Makes about 30

Notes: Ideal with green Mexican salsa (see page 86).
If you can't find fresh ravioli in sheets, individual pieces will work equally well.

Asparagus and prosciutto bundles with hollandaise

24 spears asparagus, trimmed
8 slices prosciutto, cut into thirds
   lengthways

Hollandaise
175 g (6 oz) butter
4 egg yolks
1 tablespoon lemon juice
ground white pepper

Blanch the asparagus in boiling salted water for 2 minutes, then drain and refresh in cold water. Pat dry, then cut the spears in half. Lay the bottom half of each spear next to its tip, then secure together by wrapping a piece of prosciutto around them.

To make the hollandaise, melt the butter in a small saucepan. Skim any froth off the top. Cool the butter a little. Combine the egg yolks and 2 tablespoons of water in a small heatproof bowl placed over a saucepan of simmering water, making sure the base of the bowl does not touch the water. Using a wire whisk, beat for about 3–4 minutes, or until the mixture is thick and foamy. Make sure the bowl does not get too hot or you will end up with scrambled eggs. Add the butter slowly, a little at a time at first, whisking well between each addition. Keep adding the butter in a thin stream, whisking continuously, until all the butter has been used. Try to avoid using the milky whey in the bottom of the pan, but don't worry if a little gets in. Stir in the lemon juice and season with salt and white pepper. Place in a bowl and serve warm with the asparagus.

Makes 24 bundles

Crispy Asian noodle pancakes

150 g (5½ oz) dried rice vermicelli
   noodles
15 g (¼ cup) chopped coriander
   (cilantro)
3 spring onions (scallions),
   finely sliced
1 small red chilli, finely chopped
1 stalk lemon grass, white part only,
   finely chopped
1 garlic clove, crushed
oil, for shallow-frying

Place the noodles in a bowl and cover with boiling water. Stand for 5 minutes, or until soft. Rinse under cold water, drain and dry with paper towels.

Place the noodles in a bowl with the coriander, spring onion, chilli, lemon grass and garlic. Season to taste with salt and mix.

Heat the oil in a heavy-based pan and shallow-fry 2 tablespoons of the mixture in hot oil. Flatten with a spatula while cooking and fry until crisp and golden on both sides. Drain the pancakes on paper towels and sprinkle with salt.

Makes about 25

Oyster po' boys

60 g (½ cup) self-raising flour
¼ teaspoon cayenne pepper
¼ teaspoon paprika
1 small egg
125 ml (½ cup) milk
vegetable oil, for deep-frying
18 oysters, shucked

Sift the flour, cayenne pepper, paprika and a pinch of salt into a bowl. Beat the egg and milk together and gradually add to the flour, whisking to give a smooth batter.

Fill a deep-fat fryer or large saucepan one-third full of oil and heat to 180°C (350°F), or until a cube of white bread dropped into the oil turns golden brown in 15 seconds. Pat dry the oysters, dip into the batter, and deep-fry in batches for 1–2 minutes, or until golden brown. Drain on crumpled paper towels and serve immediately either as they are or sandwiched between crusty bread.

Makes 18

Fried chickpeas

275 g (1¼ cups) dried chickpeas
oil, for deep-frying
½ teaspoon paprika
¼ teaspoon cayenne pepper

Soak the chickpeas overnight in plenty of cold water. Drain well and pat dry with paper towels.

Fill a deep saucepan one-third full of oil and heat to 180°C (350°F), or until a cube of bread dropped into the hot oil browns in 15 seconds. Deep-fry half the chickpeas for 3 minutes. Remove with a slotted spoon, drain on crumpled paper towels and repeat with the rest of the chickpeas. Partially cover the saucepan as some of the chickpeas may pop. Don't leave the oil unattended.

Deep-fry the chickpeas again in batches for 3 minutes each batch, or until browned. Drain well again on crumpled paper towels. Combine the paprika and cayenne pepper with a little salt and sprinkle the mixture over the hot chickpeas. Allow to cool before serving.

Makes a large bowl

Cheese sticks

155 g (1¼ cups) plain (all-purpose)
  flour
100 g (3½ oz) unsalted butter, chilled
  and chopped
100 g (¾ cup) grated Gruyère cheese
1 tablespoon finely chopped oregano
1 egg yolk
1 tablespoon sea salt flakes

Line two baking trays with baking paper. Put the flour and butter in a food processor and process in short bursts until the mixture resembles fine breadcrumbs. Add the Gruyère and oregano and process for 10 seconds, or until just combined. Add the egg yolk and about 1 tablespoon water, and process until the dough just comes together.

Turn the dough out onto a lightly floured surface and gather into a ball. Form 2 teaspoons of dough into a ball, then roll out into a stick about 12 cm (5 inches) long and place on the baking trays. Repeat with the remaining dough, then cover with plastic wrap and refrigerate for 15–20 minutes. Preheat the oven to 200°C (400°F/Gas 6).

Lightly brush the sticks with water and sprinkle with the sea salt flakes. Bake for 10 minutes, or until golden. Cool on a wire rack and serve with dips or as part of an antipasto platter.

Makes 30

Storage: Cheese sticks will keep for up to 1 week in an airtight container.

Heat the oils in a wok or large frying pan, add the garlic, ginger and half the spring onion, and stir-fry over high heat for 1 minute. Add the chicken and continue cooking for 3–4 minutes, or until just cooked, breaking up any lumps with a fork.

Add the water chestnuts, bamboo shoots, oyster and soy sauces, sherry, sugar and the remaining spring onion. Cook for 2–3 minutes, or until the liquid thickens a little.

Chicken san choy bau

1½ tablespoons vegetable oil
¼ teaspoon sesame oil
3 garlic cloves, crushed
3 teaspoons grated fresh ginger
6 spring onions (scallions), thinly
  sliced
500 g (1 lb 2 oz) minced (ground)
  chicken
100 g (3½ oz) drained water
  chestnuts, finely chopped
100 g (3½ oz) drained bamboo
  shoots, finely chopped
60 ml (¼ cup) oyster sauce
2 teaspoons soy sauce
60 ml (¼ cup) sherry
1 teaspoon sugar
4 small witlof (chicory/Belgian endive)
  heads, bases trimmed
oyster sauce, to serve

Allow the mixture to cool slightly before dividing among the witlof leaves; you will need about 2 heaped teaspoons per leaf. Drizzle with oyster sauce and serve immediately.

Makes about 36

Think ahead: The filling can be made up to 2 days in advance and reheated just before assembling.
Variations: Minced (ground) pork is another popular choice for san choy bau: you can either swap it directly for the minced chicken or use half of each and mix them together.
There are also several types of leaves that work well for cupping the filling. Try the small leaves from a cos or iceberg lettuce or, for a more sophisticated option, try betel leaves, available from Indian food suppliers.

Vegetable chips

500 g (1 lb 2 oz) orange sweet potato
500 g (1 lb 2 oz) beetroot
500 g (1 lb 2 oz) parsnip
oil, for deep-frying

Preheat the oven to 180°C (350°F/ Gas 4). Run a vegetable peeler along the length of the sweet potato and beetroot to make thin ribbons. Cut the parsnip into thin slices.

Fill a deep, heavy-based saucepan one-third full of oil and heat to 190°C (375°F), or until a cube of bread dropped into the oil browns in 10 seconds. Cook the vegetables in batches for about 30 seconds, or until golden and crisp, turning with tongs, if necessary. Drain on crumpled paper towels and season with salt. Keep warm on a baking tray in the oven and cook the remaining chips.

Makes a large bowl

Won ton stacks with tuna and ginger

1 1/2 tablespoons sesame seeds
12 fresh won ton wrappers
125 ml (1/2 cup) peanut or vegetable
   oil
150 g (5 1/2 oz) piece fresh tuna fillet
   (see Note)
60 g (1/4 cup) Japanese mayonnaise
50 g (1 3/4 oz) pickled ginger
50 g (1 3/4 oz) snow pea (mangetout)
   sprouts
2 teaspoons mirin
2 teaspoons soy sauce
1/4 teaspoon sugar

Think ahead: The won ton wrappers can be fried the day before serving. Store them in an airtight container with paper towels between each layer.

Lightly toast the sesame seeds in a small dry frying pan over low heat for 2–3 minutes, or until golden.

Cut the won ton wrappers into quarters to give 48 squares in total. Heat the oil in a small saucepan over medium heat and cook the wrappers in batches for 1–2 minutes, or until they are golden and crisp. Drain on crumpled paper towels.

Thinly slice the tuna into 24 slices. Spoon approximately 1/4 teaspoon of the mayonnaise onto 24 of the won ton squares. Place a slice of tuna on the mayonnaise and top with a little of the pickled ginger, snow pea sprouts and sesame seeds.

Mix the mirin, soy sauce and sugar together in a small bowl and drizzle a little over each stack. Season with pepper. Top with the remaining 24 won ton squares. Serve straight away, or the stacks will become soggy.

Makes 24

Note: For this recipe, you need good-quality tuna. Sashimi tuna is the best quality, but if you can't get that, get tuna with as little sinew as possible.

Spicy poppadoms

3 green cardamom seeds
1½ tablespoons coriander seeds
1 tablespoon cumin seeds
2 cloves
1 teaspoon black peppercorns
1 bay leaf, crushed
1 teaspoon ground mace
¼ teaspoon ground cinnamon
pinch of ground chilli
oil, for deep-frying
24 large poppadoms, broken into
    quarters

Toast the cardamom, coriander and cumin seeds, cloves, peppercorns and bay leaf in a dry frying pan over low heat for 2–3 minutes, or until richly fragrant. Cool for 5 minutes, then grind to a fine powder. Stir in the mace, cinnamon and chilli.

Fill a wide, large saucepan one-third full with oil and heat to 180°C (350°F), or until a cube of bread dropped into the oil browns in 15 seconds. Deep-fry the pieces of poppadom, a few at a time, until crisp and golden. Drain on crumpled paper towels and sprinkle with the spice mix while still hot.

Makes a large bowl

Herbed parchment bread

125 g (1 cup) plain (all-purpose) flour
2 tablespoons extra virgin olive oil
½ onion, chopped
15 g (¼ cup) fresh rosemary sprigs
15 g (¼ cup) fresh parsley
15 g (¼ cup) fresh mint leaves
2 teaspoons extra virgin olive oil, extra
sea salt

Preheat the oven to 180°C (350°F/ Gas 4). Process the flour and oil until the mixture resembles fine breadcrumbs. Transfer to a bowl.

Process the onion and herbs until finely chopped. Add 1 tablespoon of water and the extra oil and process until well combined. Add the herb mixture to the flour mixture and stir with a flat-bladed knife until it starts to come together. Add an extra tablespoon of water, if necessary. Press together and knead for 30 seconds.

Divide into 16 pieces and roll each piece between two sheets of non-stick baking paper as thinly as possible. Place on lightly greased baking trays in a single layer. Lightly brush with water and sprinkle with sea salt.

Bake each tray of breads for about 8 minutes, or until lightly browned and crisp to the touch. Transfer to wire racks to cool.

Makes 16

Cajun 'popcorn'

1 egg
250 ml (1 cup) milk
90 g (¾ cup) plain (all-purpose) flour
35 g (¼ cup) fine cornmeal
½ teaspoon baking powder
1½ teaspoons Cajun spice mix
¼ teaspoon dried basil
½ teaspoon celery salt
oil, for deep-frying
1 kg (2 lb 4 oz) prawns (shrimp),
   peeled and deveined
mayonnaise, for serving

Beat the egg and milk together. Sift the flour into a large bowl, then add the cornmeal, baking powder, Cajun spice mix, basil and celery salt. Make a well in the centre, gradually add half the beaten egg mixture and whisk until you have a smooth paste. Add the remaining egg mixture, mix well and leave to stand for 30 minutes to rest the batter and allow the starch to expand.

Fill a deep-fat fryer or large saucepan one-third full of oil and heat to 180°C (350°F), or until a cube of white bread dropped in the oil browns in 15 seconds.

Pat dry the prawns with paper towels. Dip the prawns in the batter and allow any excess batter to drain off. Cook in small batches in the oil until crisp and lightly golden. Remove with a slotted spoon or strainer and drain on crumpled paper towels. Serve hot with mayonnaise or another dipping sauce of your choice.

Serves 6

Corn muffins

310 g (2½ cups) self-raising flour
75 g (½ cup) cornmeal
250 ml (1 cup) milk
125 g (4½ oz) butter, melted
2 eggs, lightly beaten
130 g (4¾ oz) can corn kernels, drained
2 spring onions (scallions), finely chopped
60 g (½ cup) grated Cheddar cheese

Preheat the oven to 210°C (415°F/ Gas 6–7). Grease two trays of six 125 ml (½-cup) muffin holes with butter. Sift the flour and cornmeal into a large bowl and make a well in the centre.

Whisk together the milk, butter, eggs, corn, spring onion, Cheddar and salt and pepper in a separate bowl and pour into the well. Fold gently with a metal spoon until all the ingredients are just combined. Do not overmix — the mixture should still be very lumpy.

Spoon the mixture into the tin and bake for 20–25 minutes, or until lightly golden. Leave for 5 minutes before removing from the tin. Serve split in half spread with butter or cream cheese. Delicious warm or at room temperature.

Makes 12

Variation: Try adding 2 tablespoons chopped chives, 40 g (¼ cup) chopped, drained sun-dried tomato or capsicum (pepper) in oil, 2 finely chopped rashers of bacon, 2 finely chopped red chillies or ½ finely chopped red or green capsicum into the mixture with the milk and Cheddar. Another variation is to sprinkle sesame or sunflower seeds over the muffins just before baking.

Vegetable dumplings

8 dried Chinese mushrooms
1 tablespoon oil
2 teaspoons finely chopped fresh
  ginger
2 garlic cloves, crushed
100 g (3½ oz) Chinese chives, chopped
100 g (3½ oz) water spinach, cut
  into 1 cm (½ inch) lengths
60 ml (¼ cup) chicken stock
2 tablespoons oyster sauce
1 tablespoon cornflour (cornstarch)
1 teaspoon soy sauce
1 teaspoon rice wine
45 g (¼ cup) water chestnuts, chopped
chilli sauce, to serve

Wrappers
200 g (7 oz) wheat starch
1 teaspoon cornflour (cornstarch)
oil, for kneading

Soak the mushrooms in hot water for 15 minutes. Finely chop the caps. Heat the oil in a frying pan over high heat, add the ginger, garlic and a pinch of salt and white pepper. Cook for 30 seconds. Add the chives and spinach and cook for 1 minute.

Combine the stock, oyster sauce, cornflour, soy sauce and rice wine, and add to the spinach mixture with the water chestnuts and mushrooms. Cook for 1 minute, or until thickened, then cool completely.

To make the wrappers, combine the wheat starch and cornflour. Make a well and add 185 ml (¾ cup) boiling water, a little at a time, bringing the mixture together with your hands. Knead with lightly oiled hands until the dough forms a shiny ball.

Keep the dough covered while you work. Roll out walnut-sized pieces of dough into very thin 10 cm (4 inch) diameter circles. Place 1 tablespoon of filling in the centre. Pinch the edges together to form a tight ball.

Put the dumplings in a bamboo steamer lined with baking paper, leaving a gap between each one. Cover and steam for 7–8 minutes. Serve with chilli sauce.

Makes 24

Honey-roasted peanuts

350 g (12 oz) raw shelled peanuts
175 g (½ cup) honey
1½ teaspoons Chinese five-spice
powder

Preheat the oven to 150°C (300°F/
Gas 2).

Combine the ingredients in a small
saucepan and warm over low heat.

Spread the nuts onto a large baking
tray lined with baking paper and bake
for 15–20 minutes, or until golden
brown. Cool before serving.

Makes 2½ cups

Storage: You can store the honey-
roasted peanuts in an airtight
container for up to 1 week.

Blackened Cajun spiced chicken

1½ tablespoons onion powder
1½ tablespoons garlic powder
2 teaspoons paprika
1 teaspoon white pepper
2 teaspoons dried thyme
½–1 teaspoon chilli powder
8 chicken drumsticks, scored

Combine the onion powder, garlic powder, paprika, white pepper, thyme, chilli powder and 1 teaspoon salt in a plastic bag. Place the drumsticks in the bag and shake until all the pieces are coated. Leave the chicken in the fridge for at least 30 minutes to allow the flavours to develop, or overnight if time permits.

Cook the chicken on a lightly oiled barbecue grill for 55–60 minutes, or until slightly blackened and cooked through. Brush lightly with some oil to prevent drying out during cooking.

Serves 4

Mini sweet potato and leek frittatas

1 kg (2 lb 4 oz) orange sweet potato
1 tablespoon olive oil
30 g (1 oz) butter
4 leeks, white part only, thinly sliced
2 garlic cloves, crushed
250 g (1²/₃ cup) feta cheese,
   crumbled
8 eggs
125 ml (½ cup) cream

Preheat the oven to 180°C (350°F/ Gas 4). Grease twelve 125 ml (½ cup) muffin tin holes. Cut small rounds of baking paper and place into the base of each hole. Cut the sweet potato into small cubes and boil, steam or microwave until tender. Drain well and set aside.

Heat the oil and butter in a large frying pan, add the leek and cook for about 10 minutes, stirring occasionally, or until very soft and lightly golden. Add the garlic and cook for 1 minute more. Cool, then stir in the feta and sweet potato. Divide the mixture evenly among the muffin holes.

Whisk the eggs and cream together and season with salt and freshly ground black pepper. Pour the egg mixture into each hole until three-quarters filled, then press the vegetables down gently. Bake for 25–30 minutes, or until golden and set. Leave in the tins for 5 minutes, then ease out with a knife and cool on a wire rack before serving.

Makes 12

Parmesan wafers

125 g (1¼ cups) good-quality grated
  Parmesan cheese
1 tablespoon plain (all-purpose) flour
2 tablespoons thyme

Preheat the oven to 220°C (425°F/ Gas 7). Line two baking trays with baking paper and, using a 7 cm (2¾ inch) cutter as a guide, draw circles on the paper. Turn the paper upside down on the trays.

Toss the cheese and flour together in a bowl, then sprinkle 2 teaspoons of the mixture over 3–4 circles on the paper, spreading the mixture to the edge of each round. Scatter a few thyme leaves over each round.

Bake in batches for about 3 minutes, or until melted but not firm. Using a spatula, turn the rounds over and cook for a minute more, or until they are firm and light golden. Remove each round from the tray and drape over a rolling pin or bottle until cool. Repeat with the rest of the ingredients.

Makes 30

Parsnip chips

4 parsnips
oil, for deep-frying
¼ teaspoon ground cumin

Trim and peel the parsnips. Using a vegetable peeler, cut them into long, thick strips.

Fill a deep, heavy-based saucepan one-third full of oil and heat until a cube of bread dropped in the oil browns in 15 seconds. Deep-fry the parsnip strips in batches for 1 minute, or until they are golden and crisp. Remove from the oil and drain on crumpled paper towels.

Mix 2 teaspoons of salt with the cumin in a small bowl. Put the hot parsnip chips in a large bowl and season with the cumin mixture. Serve immediately.

Serves 4

Fried green tomatoes with a cornmeal crust

750 g (1 lb 10 oz) unripe, green
  tomatoes
60 g (½ cup) plain (all-purpose) flour
225 g (1½ cups) yellow cornmeal
2 teaspoons finely chopped thyme
2 teaspoons finely chopped marjoram
50 g (½ cup) grated Parmesan
  cheese
2 eggs, beaten with 1 tablespoon
  water
olive oil, for pan-frying

Preheat the oven to 180°C (350°F/
Gas 4). Cut the tomatoes into 1 cm
(½ inch) slices and season with salt.
Season the flour well with salt and
freshly ground black pepper and
place in a shallow bowl. Combine
the cornmeal, thyme, marjoram and
Parmesan. Dip the tomato slices in
the flour, coating all surfaces. Next
dip in the beaten egg, followed by the
cornmeal mixture. Set the tomatoes
aside in a single layer.

Fill a large, heavy-based frying pan
with olive oil to 5 mm (¼ inch) deep.
Heat over medium heat until a cube
of bread dropped in the oil browns
in 20 seconds. Reduce the heat a
little, then cook the tomato slices in
batches for 2–3 minutes each side,
or until golden. Remove with tongs
and drain on paper towels. Transfer
the tomato slices to a plate and keep
them warm in the oven while the rest
are being cooked. Add more oil to
the pan as necessary to maintain
the level. Serve hot.

Serves 4–6

Smoked trout sandwiches

24 thin slices brown bread
softened cream cheese, to spread
1 large telegraph cucumber, cut into
   wafer-thin slices
400 g (14 oz) good-quality smoked
   trout
2 tablespoons roughly chopped dill
lemon wedges, to garnish

Spread the bread with cream cheese.
Arrange a single layer of cucumber
on half the bread slices. Layer the
trout on top of the cucumber, then
place the other bread slices on top.
Cut off the crusts, then slice each
sandwich into four triangles.

Place the sandwiches long-edge-
down on a platter to form a pyramid.
Brush one side of the pyramid with
softened cream cheese, then sprinkle
with dill. Garnish with lemon.

Makes 48

Tempura with soy and ginger dipping sauce

200 g (7 oz) shelled large prawns (shrimp), peeled and deveined, tails intact
300 g (10½ oz) skinned haddock fillets
2 teaspoons finely grated fresh ginger
1 tablespoon mirin
100 ml (3½ fl oz) soy sauce
vegetable oil, for deep-frying
250 g (2 cups) tempura flour (see Note)
1 large egg, lightly beaten
270 ml (1 cup and 1 tablespoon) iced water

Fish substitution
bream, cod, rock cod, squid, lobster, crayfish

Make three cuts on the underside of each prawn and straighten them out. Cut the fish into bite-sized chunks.

Mix the ginger and mirin into the soy sauce, and dilute to taste with up to 2½ tablespoons of water. Pour the sauce into dipping bowls.

Fill a deep-fat fryer or large saucepan one-third full of oil and heat to 180°C (350°F), or until a cube of white bread dropped into the oil turns golden brown in 15 seconds.

Put the flour into a large bowl. Whisk the egg into the iced water. Very lightly whisk the iced water and egg into the tempura flour—it should still be lumpy. If you overwork the batter at this stage, you will not end up with a light coating. Dip the prawns and fish in the batter in batches and fry until crisp and golden. Drain on crumpled paper towels and serve immediately with the dipping sauce.

Serves 4

Note: Tempura flour is an especially fine flour available at Asian supermarkets. If you can't find it, use 185 g (1½ cups) plain (all-purpose) flour with 90 g (½ cup) rice flour.

Crumbed prawns with ponzu dipping sauce

18 raw large prawns (shrimp)
2 tablespoons cornflour (cornstarch)
3 eggs
240 g (3 cups) fresh breadcrumbs
oil, for pan-frying
80 ml (⅓ cup) ponzu sauce or 60 ml
 (¼ cup) soy sauce combined with
 1 tablespoon lemon juice

Peel and devein the prawns, leaving the tails intact. Cut down the back of each prawn to form a butterfly. Place each prawn between two layers of plastic wrap and gently beat to form a cutlet.

Put the cornflour, eggs and breadcrumbs in separate bowls. Lightly beat the eggs. Dip each prawn first into the cornflour, then into the egg and finally into the breadcrumbs, ensuring that each cutlet is well covered in crumbs.

Heat the oil in a frying pan over medium heat until hot. Cook six prawn cutlets at a time for about 1 minute each side, or until the crumbs are golden — be careful they don't burn. Serve immediately with ponzu sauce.

Makes 18

Note: Ponzu is a Japanese dipping sauce usually used for sashimi.

Bitterballen

435 ml (1¾ cups) beef stock
1 small carrot, very finely diced
½ celery stalk, very finely diced
1 small onion, very finely diced
1 bay leaf
50 g (1¾ oz) butter
50 g (1¾ oz) plain (all-purpose) flour
300 g (10½ oz) minced (ground) beef
  or veal
3 garlic cloves, crushed
1 tablespoon finely chopped parsley
1 tablespoon Worcestershire sauce
2 teaspoons ground nutmeg
1 teaspoon lemon zest, finely minced
dry breadcrumbs, to coat
3 eggs, beaten
oil, for deep-frying
English mustard, to serve

Place the stock, carrot, celery, onion and bay leaf in a saucepan and bring to the boil over high heat. Simmer for 10 minutes. Strain, reserving all the solids except the bay leaf.

Melt the butter over medium heat in a large saucepan. Add the flour, mix well and cook for 1 minute. Gradually add the warm stock, stirring constantly until you have a thick, smooth sauce. Reduce the heat to low.

Add the minced beef, garlic, parsley, Worcestershire sauce, nutmeg, lemon zest, reserved vegetables, 1 teaspoon salt and ½ teaspoon cracked black pepper. Cook over low heat for 15 minutes, stirring regularly. Cool slightly, then transfer to a clean dish. Cover and chill overnight, or until the mixture is well chilled and firm.

Roll heaped teaspoons of the mixture into balls. Roll in breadcrumbs, then in the egg, then again in breadcrumbs. Chill the finished balls as you work. Refrigerate the balls for at least 1 hour.

Fill a large heavy-based saucepan one-third full of oil and heat to 190°C (375°F), or until a cube of bread browns in 10 seconds. Deep-fry the balls for 4 minutes, or until golden. Serve immediately with mustard.

Makes about 60

Deep-fried Parmesan carrots

500 g (1 lb 2 oz) baby (dutch) carrots
60 g (½ cup) plain (all-purpose) flour
2 teaspoons ground cumin
2 eggs
250 g (3 cups) fine fresh white breadcrumbs
1 tablespoon chopped parsley
65 g (²/₃ cup) finely grated Parmesan cheese
oil, for deep-frying

Trim the leafy carrot tops, leaving about 2 cm (¾ inch), and wash the carrots. Bring a large saucepan of water to the boil, add 1 teaspoon of salt and cook the carrots for 5 minutes, or until tender (test with a metal skewer). Drain, dry well with paper towels and leave to cool.

Sift the flour and cumin onto a sheet of greaseproof paper, then beat the eggs together in a wide, shallow bowl. Combine the breadcrumbs, parsley and Parmesan, and season with salt and pepper. Roll the carrots in the flour, then the eggs and finally the breadcrumbs. For an extra crispy coating repeat this process.

Fill a deep, heavy-based saucepan one-third full of oil and heat until a cube of bread dropped into the oil browns in 20 seconds. Deep-fry the carrots in batches until golden and crisp. Serve immediately.

Serves 6

Curried nuts

500 g (1 lb 2 oz) mixed nuts
  (almonds, brazil nuts, pecans,
  macadamias, cashew nuts)
1 egg white
2 tablespoons curry powder
1 teaspoon ground cumin

Preheat the oven to 150°C (300°F/ Gas 2). Spread the nuts in a single layer on a baking tray and roast for 10 minutes.

Whisk the egg white until frothy, then add the nuts, curry powder, cumin and 1 teaspoon salt. Toss together and return to the oven for a further 10–15 minutes, then allow to cool.

Makes 4 1/2 cups

Scallops on potato crisps with pea purée

1 tablespoon butter
3 French shallots, finely chopped
1 garlic clove, finely chopped
2 slices mild pancetta, finely chopped
155 g (1 cup) frozen peas
60 ml (¼ cup) chicken stock or water
oil, for deep-frying, plus 1 tablespoon
4–5 floury potatoes (e.g. russet, King
   Edward), peeled and very thinly
   sliced to get 48 slices
24 scallops, cut in half horizontally
   through the centre
mint, to garnish

Think ahead: The purée can be made
2 days early and refrigerated. The
potato crisps can be cooked 2 hours
early; store in an airtight container.

Melt the butter in a small saucepan
and fry the shallots, garlic and
pancetta over low heat for 3 minutes,
or until soft but not coloured. Add
the peas and stock, and cook over
high heat for 3 minutes, or until all
the liquid has evaporated. Cool a
little, transfer to a food processor
and purée until smooth. Season.

Fill a deep heavy-based saucepan or
deep-fryer one-third full of oil and heat
to 190°C (375°F), or until a cube of
bread dropped into the oil browns in
10 seconds. Cook the potato slices in
batches until crisp and golden. Drain
on crumpled paper towels and
sprinkle with salt.

Toss the scallops with 1 tablespoon
oil. Season lightly. Heat a chargrill
pan or barbecue hotplate to hot, then
sear the scallops in batches for
5 seconds each side, or until lightly
browned but opaque in the middle.

Reheat the pea purée. Dollop
1 teaspoon of purée on each potato
crisp, then top with a scallop. Season
with pepper and garnish with mint.

Makes 48

Stuffed baby calamari with lime and chilli dipping sauce

Dipping sauce
80 ml (⅓ cup) lime juice
60 ml (¼ cup) fish sauce
2 tablespoons grated palm sugar
  or soft brown sugar
1 small red chilli, finely sliced into rounds

12 medium squid
12 raw prawns (shrimp), peeled,
  deveined and chopped
150 g (5½ oz) minced (ground) pork
4 garlic cloves, crushed
½ teaspoon finely grated fresh ginger
3 teaspoons fish sauce
2 teaspoons lime juice
1 teaspoon grated palm sugar
2 tablespoons chopped coriander
  (cilantro) leaves
peanut oil, for brushing

For the dipping sauce, put the lime juice, fish sauce, palm sugar and chilli in a bowl and stir it together until the sugar has dissolved. Cover the bowl.

Gently pull the tentacles away from the tube of the squid (the intestines should come away at the same time). Remove the quill from inside the body and discard, as well as any white membrane. Pull the skin away from the hood under running water, then cut the tentacles away from the intestines and give them a rinse to remove the sucker rings. Finely chop the tentacles to add to the stuffing.

Put the prawns, pork, garlic, ginger, fish sauce, juice, sugar, coriander and chopped tentacles in a bowl and mix together. Use a teaspoon to put the stuffing in each tube and push it to the bottom, then secure the hole with a toothpick. Don't overfill the tubes as the stuffing will expand when cooked.

Preheat the chargrill plate to medium direct heat, brush the squid tubes with peanut oil, and barbecue them for 8 minutes, or until cooked, turning when the flesh becomes opaque and slightly charred. Remove the tooth-picks and cut each tube into thin rounds. Serve with the dipping sauce.

Serves 4

Pesto bagel chips

4 three-day-old plain bagels
125 g (½ cup) ready-made pesto
100 g (1 cup) shredded Parmesan
  cheese

Preheat the oven to 170°C (325°F/ Gas 3). Slice each bagel into 6 thin rings.

Bake on a baking tray for 10 minutes. Brush with pesto and sprinkle with shredded Parmesan. Bake for a further 5 minutes, or until the chips are lightly golden.

Makes 24

Basil mussels

1 kg (2 lb 4 oz) black mussels
10 g (¼ oz) butter
2 red Asian shallots, chopped
125 ml (½ cup) dry white wine

Basil butter
50 g (1¾ oz) butter
10 g (⅓ cup) basil leaves
1 garlic clove, chopped
2 tablespoons dry breadcrumbs

Scrub the mussels with a stiff brush and pull out the hairy beards. Discard any broken mussels or open ones that don't close when tapped on the bench. Rinse well.

Melt the butter in a large saucepan over medium heat. Add the shallots and cook for 2 minutes, or until soft. Add the wine and mussels, increase the heat and cook for 4–5 minutes, stirring occasionally, until the mussels have opened. Remove the open mussels and discard unopened ones.

For the basil butter, process all the ingredients together in a food processor or blender until smooth. Season with ground black pepper.

Separate the mussel shells, leaving the meat on one half. Discard the empty shells. Place a teaspoon of basil butter on each mussel. Arrange on a foil-lined grill (broiler) tray and cook under a hot grill for 1 minute, or until the butter is melted. Season with salt and ground black pepper, to taste.

Serves 6

Rösti with smoked trout and salsa verde

1 small smoked trout
450 g (1 lb) floury potatoes (e.g.
 russet, King Edward or pontiac)
2 spring onions (scallions), thinly
 sliced
80 ml (⅓ cup) olive oil

Salsa verde
30 g (1½ cups) flat-leaf (Italian)
 parsley
30 g (1 cup) basil leaves
1 tablespoon capers, drained
1 tablespoon chopped gherkin or
 4 cornichons (baby gherkins)
2 anchovies, drained
1 garlic clove, chopped
2 teaspoons Dijon mustard
60 ml (¼ cup) olive oil
1 tablespoon lemon juice

Remove the skin from the trout, pull the flesh from the bones and flake into pieces.

To make the salsa verde, place the parsley, basil, capers, gherkin, anchovies, garlic and mustard in a food processor and blend until finely chopped. While the motor is running, blend in the oil and lemon juice until mixed together. Season with pepper.

To make the rösti, peel and coarsely grate the potatoes. Squeeze out as much liquid as possible. Mix the flesh in a bowl with the spring onion. Heat the oil in a large heavy-based frying pan over medium–high heat. To cook the rösti, take heaped teaspoons of the potato mixture, add to the pan in batches and press down with a spatula to help the potato stay together. Cook for 2–3 minutes each side, or until crisp and golden. Drain on crumpled paper towels.

Top each rösti with a teaspoon of salsa verde then some flakes of trout. Serve warm or at room temperature.

Makes 32

Think ahead: The rösti can be made 8 hours beforehand and kept in an airtight container lined with paper towels. Reheat for 5 minutes in a 180°C (350°F/Gas 4) oven.

Steamed prawn banana leaf cups

16 x 10 cm (4 inch) circles of banana
   leaf or 8 cups each with a 100 ml
   (3½ fl oz) capacity
300 g (10½ oz) prawns (shrimp),
   peeled and deveined
1 small red chilli, deseeded
2 teaspoons red curry paste
3 cm (1¼ inch) piece of lemon grass,
   roughly chopped
1 large egg
60 ml (¼ cup) coconut cream
1 tablespoon fish sauce
¼ teaspoon sugar
2 tablespoons unsalted peanuts

Begin by making eight banana leaf
cups. Place two banana leaf circles
together to make a double layer.
Make four small tucks around the
circle, stapling them to secure as
you go, to create a banana leaf 'cup'.
Repeat for the other seven cups.
Alternatively you can use eight 100 ml
(3½ fl oz) ramekins. Either way, also
cut out eight 7 cm (2¾ inch) circles of
baking paper.

Tip the prawns into a food processor
with the chilli, curry paste, lemon
grass, egg, coconut cream, fish
sauce, sugar and half of the peanuts.
Blend to a rough paste.

Evenly divide the mixture among the
cups. Place a circle of baking paper
on the top of each one. Place in a
bamboo or metal steamer, cover and
steam for 10–12 minutes, or until the
mixture has risen and feels firm to the
touch. You may need to cook in two
batches. Remove the baking paper.

Meanwhile, lightly toast the remaining
peanuts. Cool a little, then roughly
chop. Serve each cup with a little of
the toasted peanuts scattered over
the top.

Makes 8

Seasoned popcorn

60 ml (¼ cup) oil
150 g (5½ oz) popping corn
40 g (1½ oz) butter
125 g (⅔ cup) finely chopped
   Kalamata olives
1 bird's eye chilli, finely chopped
1 garlic clove, crushed
1 tablespoon chopped parsley
1 tablespoon chopped oregano
1 teaspoon grated lemon zest

Heat the oil in a large saucepan, add the popping corn and cover. Cook over medium heat, shaking occasionally, until the popping stops. Transfer to a large bowl and discard any unpopped corn.

Melt the butter in a large frying pan and add the remaining ingredients. Mix, then toss through the popcorn. Serve warm.

Makes a large bowl

Sweet potato and lentil pastry pouches

2 tablespoons olive oil
1 large leek, finely chopped
2 garlic cloves, crushed
125 g (4½ oz) button mushrooms, roughly chopped
2 teaspoons ground cumin
2 teaspoons ground coriander
95 g (½ cup) brown or green lentils
125 g (½ cup) red lentils
500 ml (2 cups) vegetable stock
300 g (10½ oz) sweet potato, diced
4 tablespoons finely chopped coriander (cilantro) leaves
8 sheets ready-rolled puff pastry
1 egg, lightly beaten
½ leek, extra, cut into 5 mm (¼ inch) wide strips
200 g (7 oz) plain yoghurt
2 tablespoons grated Lebanese (short) cucumber
½ teaspoon soft brown sugar

Preheat the oven to 200°C (400°F/ Gas 6). Heat the oil in a saucepan over medium heat and cook the leek for 2–3 minutes, or until soft. Add the garlic, mushrooms, cumin and ground coriander and cook for 1 minute, or until fragrant.

Add the combined lentils and stock and bring to the boil. Reduce the heat and simmer for 20–25 minutes, or until the lentils are cooked through, stirring occasionally. Add the sweet potato in the last 5 minutes.

Transfer to a bowl and stir in the coriander. Season to taste. Cool.

Cut the pastry sheets into four even squares. Place 1½ tablespoons of filling into the centre of each square and bring the edges together to form a pouch. Pinch together, then tie each pouch with string. Lightly brush with egg and place on lined baking trays. Bake for 20–25 minutes, or until the pastry is puffed and golden.

Soak the leek strips in boiling water for 30 seconds. Remove the string and re-tie with a piece of blanched leek. Put the yoghurt, cucumber and sugar in a bowl and mix together well. Serve with the pastry pouches.

Makes 32

Basil and cheese grissini

7 g (¼ oz) sachet dry yeast
1 teaspoon sugar
500 g (4 cups) plain (all-purpose) flour
60 ml (¼ cup) olive oil
15 g (¼ cup) chopped basil
50 g (½ cup) finely grated Parmesan
  cheese
2 teaspoons sea salt flakes

Combine the yeast, sugar and
315 ml (1¼ cups) warm water in a
bowl and leave in a warm place for
5–10 minutes, or until foamy. Sift the
flour and 1 teaspoon salt into a bowl.
Stir the yeast and oil into the flour to
form a dough, adding a little more
water if necessary.

Gently gather the dough into a ball
and turn out onto a lightly floured
surface. Knead for 10 minutes, or
until soft and elastic. Add the basil
and Parmesan, and knead for
1–2 minutes to incorporate evenly.

Place the dough in a lightly oiled bowl
and cover with plastic wrap. Leave
in a warm place for 1 hour, or until
doubled in volume. Preheat the oven
to 230°C (450°F/Gas 8) and lightly
grease two large baking trays.

Punch down the dough and knead
for 1 minute. Divide into 24 portions,
and roll each portion into a 30 cm
(12 inch) long stick. Place on the trays
and brush with water. Sprinkle with
the salt flakes. Bake for 15 minutes,
or until crisp and golden.

Makes 24

Prawn sushi cones

330 g (1½ cups) sushi rice or
   short-grain rice
2 tablespoons seasoned rice vinegar
1 avocado
1 small Lebanese (short) cucumber
8 sheets nori, cut in half on
   the diagonal
1 teaspoon wasabi paste
80 g (2¾ oz) pickled ginger
16 cooked medium prawns (shrimp),
   peeled and deveined
soy sauce, to serve

Place the rice in a sieve and rinse under cold running water. Set aside to drain for 1 hour. Place the drained rice in a large saucepan and add 375 ml (1½ cups) water. Cover and bring to the boil, then reduce the heat to very low and cook, tightly covered, for 15 minutes. Remove from the heat and leave the lid on for 10 minutes.

Transfer the rice to a large shallow bowl and drizzle with the vinegar. Fold the vinegar through the rice, tossing lightly with a large metal spoon or spatula to cool as you combine. Do not use a stirring action; it will make the rice mushy.

Quarter and peel the avocado and cut each quarter into four long wedges. Trim the ends of the cucumber, then cut lengthways into 16 strips.

Hold a sheet of nori shiny-side-down, flat in your hand. Place 2 tablespoons of rice on the left-hand side and spread out over half the nori sheet. Dab with a little wasabi and top with some pickled ginger. Place a strip each of avocado and cucumber on the rice and top with one prawn. Roll up the nori to form a cone, enclosing the smaller end. Repeat, using all the ingredients. Serve with soy sauce.

Makes 16

Scallop ceviche

16 scallops, in their shells, cleaned
1 teaspoon finely grated lime zest
60 ml (¹/₄ cup) lime juice
2 garlic cloves, chopped
2 red chillies, deseeded and chopped
1 tablespoon chopped coriander
   (cilantro) leaves
1 tablespoon olive oil
whole coriander (cilantro) leaves,
   for serving

Take the scallops off their shells, but don't throw away the shells.

In a non-metallic bowl, mix together the lime zest and juice, garlic, chilli, chopped coriander and the olive oil, and season with salt and pepper. Put the scallops in the dressing and stir to coat. Cover with plastic wrap and refrigerate for 2 hours. The acid from the lime juice will 'cold-cook' the scallop meat, turning it white.

To serve, slide each scallop back onto a half shell and spoon a little of the lime dressing over each of the scallops. Top each one with a coriander leaf. Serve cold.

Serves 4

Mandarin and duck rice paper rolls

1 whole Chinese roast duck
24 small Vietnamese rice paper
  wrappers
3 mandarins, peeled and segmented
20 g (1 cup) mint
60 g (2¼ oz) chives, cut into 3–4 cm
  (1¼–1½ inch) lengths
2 tablespoons hoisin sauce
2 tablespoons fresh mandarin juice

Remove the flesh and skin from the duck and shred into 1 cm x 3 cm (½ inch x 1¼ inch) pieces.

Working with one wrapper at a time, briefly soak each wrapper in cold water until softened, then place on a dry tea towel. Arrange 2–3 pieces of duck at the end of the wrapper closest to you. Top with 2 segments of mandarin, 3 mint leaves and several lengths of chives. Fold the end closest to you over the filling, fold in the sides and firmly roll up the rice paper to form a small spring roll.

Combine the hoisin sauce and mandarin juice in a bowl and serve as a dipping sauce with the rice paper rolls. These are best served immediately as the rolls will start to dry out if left for too long.

Makes 24

Mini steak sandwiches

100 ml (3½ fl oz) olive oil
1 onion, thinly sliced
15 g (¾ cup) parsley
10 large basil leaves
20 mint leaves
1 garlic clove, crushed
1 tablespoon Dijon mustard
1 tablespoon capers
2 anchovy fillets
400 g (14 oz) fillet steak, about 1 cm
  (½ inch) thick
1 baguette, cut into 40 x 5 mm
  (¼ inch) slices

Heat 2 tablespoons of oil in a frying pan and cook the onion over low heat for 25 minutes, or until caramelized.

To make the salsa verde, place the parsley, basil, mint, garlic, mustard, capers, anchovies and the remaining oil in a food processor and pulse to a thick paste. Season.

Cut out 20 rounds from the steak with a 2.5 cm (1 inch) cutter. Season, then sear on a lightly oiled chargrill pan or barbecue hotplate on both sides for 1–2 minutes, or until cooked to your liking. Put a little of the onion on 20 rounds of bread, top with a piece of steak and a dollop of salsa verde, then top with the remaining bread. Serve warm.

Makes 20

Sigara boregi

500 g (1 lb 2 oz) English spinach
  leaves
1 tablespoon olive oil
4 garlic cloves, crushed
200 g (7 oz) French shallots, finely
  chopped
75 g (½ cup) crumbled feta cheese
1 egg, lightly beaten
3 tablespoons chopped flat-leaf
  (Italian) parsley
¼ teaspoon finely grated lemon zest
¼ teaspoon paprika
pinch of nutmeg
6 sheets filo pastry
125 g (4½ oz) butter, melted
light olive oil, for deep-frying

Wash the spinach, leaving it quite
wet. Place in a saucepan, cover and
cook over low heat until just wilted.
Tip the spinach into a colander and
press out the liquid with a wooden
spoon. When cool, squeeze dry.

Heat the oil in a frying pan, and cook
the garlic and shallots for 2 minutes,
or until soft but not browned. Transfer
to a bowl and add the feta cheese,
egg, parsley, spinach and lemon zest.
Season with the paprika, nutmeg and
salt and pepper, and mix well.

Brush a sheet of filo with melted
butter, then fold it in half lengthways. It
should measure about 32 cm x 12 cm
(13 inches x 5 inches). Cut in half
widthways. Brush with butter, place
1 heaped tablespoon of filling at one
end of each piece and spread to within
1 cm (½ inch) of each side. Fold in the
sides to cover the edges of the filling,
continuing the folds right up the length
of the pastry. Brush with melted butter,
then roll up tightly. Brush the outside
with butter and seal. Cover with a damp
tea towel while you prepare the rest.

Heat the light olive oil in a deep frying
pan to 180°C (350°F), or until a cube
of bread browns in 15 seconds.
Deep-fry in batches until golden.

Makes 12

Prawn potstickers

Dipping sauce
60 ml (¼ cup) soy sauce
1 spring onion (scallion), thinly sliced
1 garlic clove, crushed
¼ teaspoon finely chopped fresh
    ginger
¼ teaspoon sesame oil

500 g (1 lb 2 oz) raw medium prawns
    (shrimp)
40 g (1½ oz) Chinese cabbage, finely
    shredded
40 g (1½ oz) drained water chestnuts,
    finely chopped
1 tablespoon finely chopped
    coriander (cilantro) leaves
24 round gow gee wrappers
    (see Note)
1 tablespoon vegetable oil
125 ml (½ cup) chicken stock

To make the dipping sauce, mix together all the ingredients in a small bowl.

Peel and devein the prawns, then finely chop. Combine the prawn meat, cabbage, water chestnuts and coriander.

Lay out all the gow gee wrappers on a work surface and put one heaped teaspoon of the prawn filling in the centre of each. Moisten the edges with water and draw together into the shape of a moneybag, pressing the edges together firmly to seal.

Heat the oil in a large frying pan and add the potstickers. Cook in batches over medium heat for 2 minutes, or until just brown on the bottom. Add the stock, then quickly cover with a lid as it will spit. Steam for 2–3 minutes, taking care that all the stock does not evaporate and the potstickers do not burn. Serve immediately with the dipping sauce.

Makes 24

Note: Gow gee wrappers are rolled out round pieces of dough made from wheat flour and water. They are available from Asian food stores.

Cheese, olive and sun-dried tomato toasts

250 g (2 cups) self-raising flour
125 g (1 cup) grated Cheddar cheese
25 g (¼ cup) freshly grated Parmesan
   cheese
50 g (⅓ cup) pine nuts
250 ml (1 cup) milk
1 egg, lightly beaten
30 g (1 oz) butter, melted
60 g (½ cup) pitted black olives,
   chopped
40 g (¼ cup) sun-dried tomatoes,
   finely chopped
40 g (⅓ cup) grated Cheddar cheese,
   extra

Preheat the oven to 200°C (400°F/
Gas 6). Lightly grease two 8 cm x
26 cm (3 inch x 10½ inch) bar tins and
cover the bases with non-stick baking
paper. Combine the flour, cheeses and
pine nuts in a bowl. Make a well in the
centre of the mixture.

Pour in the combined milk, egg,
butter, olives and sun-dried tomato,
and stir to form a slightly sticky dough.

Divide the mixture between the tins.
Smooth the surface and sprinkle with
the extra cheese. Bake for 45 minutes,
or until cooked through when tested
with a skewer. Leave in the tins for
5 minutes, then turn onto wire racks
to cool.

Cut into 5 mm (¼ inch) slices and
place on baking trays lined with baking
paper. Bake for 15–20 minutes, or until
the toasts are golden and crisp.

Makes about 50

Polenta wedges with bocconcini and tomato

1 tablespoon olive oil
250 g (1²/₃ cups) polenta
75 g (¾ cup) grated Parmesan
  cheese
2¹/₂ tablespoons ready-made pesto
150 g (5¹/₂ oz) bocconcini, thinly
  sliced
12 cherry tomatoes, cut into quarters
15 g (¹/₂ cup) basil, larger leaves torn

Lightly grease a 20 cm x 30 cm (8 inch x 12 inch) baking tin with the olive oil. Bring 1 litre (4 cups) lightly salted water to the boil in a saucepan. Once the water is boiling, add the polenta in a steady stream, stirring continuously to prevent lumps forming. Reduce the heat to very low and simmer, stirring regularly, for about 20–25 minutes, or until the polenta starts to come away from the side of the pan.

Stir the Parmesan into the polenta and season with salt and pepper. Spoon the polenta into the baking tray, smooth the top with the back of a wet spoon and leave for 1 hour.

Once the polenta has set, carefully tip it out onto a board and cut into 24 x 5 cm (2 inch) squares, then cut each square into two triangles. Chargrill the polenta in batches on a preheated chargrill pan or barbecue hotplate for 2–3 minutes on each side, or until warmed through.

Spread each triangle with 1 teaspoon of the pesto, top with a slice of bocconcini and a tomato quarter. Season and grill (broil) for 1–2 minutes, or until the cheese starts to melt. Garnish with basil.

Makes 48

Mini spicy pork quesadillas

2³/₄ tablespoons olive oil
¹/₂ teaspoon ground oregano
1 teaspoon ground cumin
¹/₂ teaspoon garlic salt
¹/₂ teaspoon cayenne pepper
350 g (12 oz) minced (ground) pork
2–3 chopped jalapeño chillies in brine
30 g (¹/₄ cup) pitted black olives,
  sliced
55 g (¹/₃ cup) green olives stuffed with
  red pimentos, sliced
2 tablespoons chopped coriander
  (cilantro) leaves
12 x 16 cm (6¹/₂ inch) flour tortillas
60 g (¹/₂ cup) grated mild Cheddar
  cheese
75 g (¹/₂ cup) grated mozzarella
  cheese
coriander (cilantro) sprigs, to garnish

To make the spicy pork mince, heat
1¹/₂ tablespoons of the olive oil in a
large frying pan; when hot add the
oregano, cumin, garlic salt and cayenne
pepper and cook for 30 seconds. Add
the minced pork and cook over high
heat for 10 minutes, before incorporat-
ing the chillies and all the olives. Cook
for another 5 minutes, then stir in the
chopped coriander. Remove from the
heat and allow -to cool.

Cut each tortilla in half. Place
1 tablespoon of filling on one half of
each half. Mix the grated cheeses
together, then put 1 tablespoon of
the cheese on top of the spicy pork
mince. Turn the flap of tortilla over
the filling and press down firmly.

Heat 2 teaspoons of the remaining
oil in a non-stick frying pan over high
heat and cook the quesadillas in
batches of six for 3–4 minutes each
side, or until golden. Add a teaspoon
of oil to the pan after each batch.
Garnish with coriander sprigs.

Makes 24

Variation: For a very simple vegetarian
filling, simply sprinkle each half tortilla
with 1 tablespoon chopped tomato,
chilli, olives and coriander, then the
cheese; fold over and cook as for the
pork quesadillas.

Steamed pork buns

250 ml (1 cup) milk
125 g (½ cup) caster (superfine) sugar
450 g (3 cups) char siu pork bun flour
 (available from Asian food stores)
1 tablespoon oil

Filling
2 teaspoons oil
1 garlic clove, crushed
2 spring onions (scallions), finely
 chopped
3 teaspoons cornflour (cornstarch)
2 teaspoons hoisin sauce
1½ teaspoons soy sauce
½ teaspoon caster (superfine) sugar
150 g (5½ oz) Chinese barbecued
 (char siu) pork, finely chopped

Combine the milk and sugar, and stir over low heat until dissolved. Sift all but two tablespoons of flour into a bowl and make a well. Gradually add the milk, stirring until it just comes together. Dust a work surface with the reserved flour and knead the dough for 10 minutes, or until elastic. Knead the oil into the dough a little at a time, kneading for 10 minutes. Cover with plastic wrap and chill for 30 minutes.

For the filling, heat the oil in a pan, add the garlic and spring onion and stir over medium heat until just soft. Blend the cornflour with 80 ml (⅓ cup) water, the sauces and sugar, and add to the pan. Stir over medium heat until the mixture boils and thickens. Remove from the heat and stir in the pork. Allow to cool.

Divide the dough into 24 portions and flatten, so the edges are thinner than the centre. Place teaspoons of filling on each and pull up the edges around the filling, pinching firmly to seal. Place each bun on a square of greaseproof paper and place 3 cm (1¼ inches) apart in a bamboo steamer. Steam in batches for 15 minutes, or until the buns have risen and are cooked through.

Makes about 24

Prawns in Chinese pancakes

24 raw medium prawns (shrimp), peeled and deveined
80 ml (⅓ cup) Chinese rice wine or dry sherry
2 tablespoons soy sauce
2 teaspoons sesame oil
2 tablespoons vegetable oil
4 garlic cloves, finely chopped
1 cm x 4 cm (½ inch x 1½ inch) piece fresh ginger, peeled and finely shredded
120–160 ml (4–5 fl oz) Chinese plum sauce
2 teaspoons chilli sauce
2 spring onions (scallions), finely chopped
24 Chinese pancakes (Available in the freezer of Asian food stores)
1 small Lebanese (short) cucumber, peeled, seeded and cut into thin 5 cm (2 inch) long strips
12 garlic chives, cut into 5 cm (2 inch) lengths

Place the prawns in a non-metallic bowl with the rice wine, soy sauce and sesame oil and marinate for at least 10 minutes.

Heat a wok over high heat, add the vegetable oil and swirl to coat. Add the garlic and ginger and sauté for 1–2 minutes. Use a slotted spoon or tongs to remove the prawns from the marinade and add them to the wok. Reserve the marinade. Stir the prawns for 2 minutes, or until they start to turn pink, then add the plum sauce, chilli sauce and the reserved marinade. Stir-fry for 2–3 minutes, or until the prawns are cooked, curled and slightly glazed. Remove from the heat and stir in the spring onion.

Place the pancakes in a non-stick frying pan over medium heat for 1 minute, or until warm.

To assemble, put a prawn, a few slices of cucumber and a few chive pieces on each pancake, spoon on some sauce, then fold over. Serve immediately.

Makes 24

Crispy bread fingers

2 tablespoons sweet chilli sauce
1 tablespoon peanut oil
1 loaf Turkish bread

Combine the sweet chilli sauce and peanut oil.

Cut the bread in half. Brush the top and bottom with the oil mixture.

Place on an oven tray and grill (broil) for 1–2 minutes, or until crispy and golden. Cut into 2 cm (³⁄₄ inch) fingers.

Makes about 50

Chermoula prawns

Chermoula
80 ml (⅓ cup) virgin olive oil
3 tablespoons chopped coriander
  (cilantro) leaves
2 tablespoons chopped flat-leaf
  (Italian) parsley
2 tablespoons chopped preserved
  lemon zest
2 tablespoons lemon juice
2 garlic cloves, chopped
1 small red chilli, seeded and finely
  chopped
1 teaspoon ground cumin
½ teaspoon paprika

20 raw medium prawns (shrimp)
370 g (2 cups) instant couscous
375 ml (1½ cups) boiling chicken
  stock
1 tablespoon olive oil
2 tablespoons shredded mint leaves

Process the chermoula ingredients to a coarse purée, then season with salt.

Peel and devein the prawns, keeping the tails intact. Thread a cocktail stick through the body of each prawn to keep them straight, then place them in a dish and spoon the chermoula over them, turning to coat. Chill the prawns, covered, for 30 minutes, turning occasionally.

Place the couscous in a heatproof bowl, pour on the boiling stock and oil, cover and leave for 3–4 minutes. Fluff the couscous with a fork and stir in the mint.

Arrange the prawns on a foil-lined grill tray and cook under a hot grill (broiler) for 2–3 minutes each side, or until pink and cooked. Divide the couscous and prawns among four plates.

Serves 4

Dressed-up baby potatoes

24 even bite-sized new potatoes,
   washed and dried
80 ml (⅓ cup) olive oil
1 tablespoon drained capers, patted
   dry
1 rasher bacon
1 tablespoon cream
10 g (¼ oz) butter
125 g (½ cup) sour cream
1 tablespoon chopped chives
1 tablespoon red or black fish roe

Preheat the oven to 180°C (350°F/
Gas 4). Line a baking tray with baking
paper. Place the potatoes in a bowl
and toss with half the olive oil.
Sprinkle with salt and black pepper,
then put on the baking tray and bake
for 40 minutes, or until cooked
through, rotating them 2–3 times
so that they brown evenly.

Meanwhile, heat the remaining oil in a
frying pan and cook the capers over
high heat, or until they open into small
flowers. Drain on paper towels. Cook
the bacon under a hot grill (broiler)
until crispy. Cool, then finely chop.

Remove the potatoes from the oven.
When cool enough to handle, cut a
thin lid from each potato. Discard the
lids. Use a melon baller or small
teaspoon to scoop out the flesh from
the middle of the potatoes, leaving a
1 cm (½ inch) border. Put the potato
flesh in a bowl and mash thoroughly
with the cream, butter and salt and
black pepper. Spoon the mash back
into the potatoes.

Top each potato with a small dollop of
sour cream. Divide the potatoes into
four groups of six and use a separate
topping for each group: capers,
bacon, chives and fish roe.

Makes 24

Arancini

440 g (2 cups) risotto rice
1 egg, lightly beaten
1 egg yolk
50 g (½ cup) grated Parmesan cheese
plain (all-purpose) flour
2 eggs, lightly beaten
dry breadcrumbs, to coat
oil, for deep-frying

Meat sauce
1 dried porcini mushroom
1 tablespoon olive oil
1 onion, chopped
125 g (4½ oz) minced (ground) beef
   or veal
2 slices prosciutto, finely chopped
2 tablespoons tomato paste (purée)
80 ml (⅓ cup) white wine
½ teaspoon dried thyme leaves
3 tablespoons finely chopped parsley

Cook the rice in boiling water for
20 minutes, or until just soft. Drain,
without rinsing, and cool. Put in
a large bowl and add the egg, egg
yolk and Parmesan. Stir until the rice
sticks together. Cover and set aside.

To make the meat sauce, soak the
mushroom in hot water for 10 minutes
to soften, then squeeze dry and chop
finely. Heat the oil in a frying pan. Add
the mushroom and onion and cook
for 3 minutes, or until soft. Add the
mince, stirring until browned. Add the
prosciutto, tomato paste, wine, thyme
and pepper to taste. Cook, stirring,
(5 mins) until all the liquid is absorbed.
Add the parsley and set aside to cool.

With wet hands, form the rice mixture
into 10 balls. Wet your hands again
and gently pull the balls apart. Place
3 teaspoons of the meat sauce in the
centre of each. Reshape to enclose
the filling. Roll in the flour, beaten egg
and breadcrumbs and chill for 1 hour.

Fill a deep heavy-based pan one-third
full of oil and heat to 180°C (350°F),
or until a cube of bread browns in
15 seconds. Deep-fry the croquettes,
two at a time, for 3–4 minutes, or until
golden brown. Drain on paper towels
and keep warm while cooking the rest.

Makes 10

Cocktail leek pies

60 g (2¼ oz) butter
2 tablespoons olive oil
1 onion, finely chopped
3 leeks, finely sliced
1 garlic clove, chopped
1 tablespoon plain (all-purpose) flour
2 tablespoons sour cream
100 g (1 cup) grated Parmesan
  cheese
1 teaspoon chopped thyme
4 sheets frozen puff pastry, defrosted
1 egg, lightly beaten

Heat the butter and oil in a large frying pan over medium heat. Add the onion and cook, stirring occasionally, for 2 minutes. Add the leek and garlic and cook for 5 minutes, or until the leek is softened and lightly coloured. Add the flour and stir into the mixture for 1 minute. Add the sour cream and stir until slightly thickened. Transfer to a bowl and add the Parmesan and thyme. Season with salt and cracked black pepper and allow to cool.

Preheat the oven to 200°C (400°F/Gas 6). Place a lightly greased baking tray in the oven to heat. Using a 6 cm (2½ inch) cutter, cut the pastry into 64 circles. Place 2 heaped teaspoons of filling on half the pastry circles, leaving a small border. Lightly brush the edges with egg, then place a pastry circle on top of each. Seal the edges well with a fork. Lightly brush the tops with egg. Place the pies on the heated tray and bake for 25 minutes, or until the pies are puffed and golden.

Makes 32

Prawn, noodle and nori parcels

Dipping sauce
80 ml (1/3 cup) tonkatsu sauce or
  barbecue sauce
2 tablespoons lemon juice
1 tablespoon sake or mirin
1–2 teaspoons grated fresh ginger

250 g (9 oz) dried somen noodles
3 sheets nori (dried seaweed)
60 g (1/2 cup) plain (all-purpose) flour
2 egg yolks
24 raw medium prawns (shrimp),
  peeled and deveined with
  the tails intact
oil, for deep-frying

Combine the dipping sauce ingredients, adding the ginger to taste.

Using a sharp knife, cut the noodles to the same length as the prawns (from the head to the base of the tail). Keep the noodles in neat bundles. Cut the nori into 2.5 cm (1 inch) wide strips.

Sift the flour and make a well in the centre. Mix the egg yolks with 60 ml (1/4 cup) of water. Gradually add to the flour, whisking to make a smooth batter. Add another tablespoon of water if the mixture is too thick.

Dip a prawn in the batter, letting the excess run off. Roll the prawn lengthways in noodles to coat it with a single layer. Keep the noodles in place by rolling a nori strip around the centre of the prawn and securing it with a little batter. Repeat with the rest of the prawns.

Fill a deep heavy-based saucepan or deep-fryer one-third full of oil and heat to 180°C (350°F), or until a cube of bread browns in 15 seconds. Deep-fry 2–3 prawns at a time, for about 1–2 minutes, or until the prawns are cooked. Drain on crumpled paper towels and keep warm. Serve warm with the dipping sauce.

Makes 24

Gyoza

300 g (10½ oz) minced (ground) pork
250 g (9 oz) finely shredded and
    lightly blanched Chinese cabbage
    with the excess water squeezed out
60 g (2¼ oz) Chinese chives,
    chopped
1 tablespoon finely chopped fresh
    ginger
60 ml (¼ cup) soy sauce
1 tablespoon rice wine
1 teaspoon sugar
45 gow gee wrappers
2 teaspoons oil

Dipping sauce
2 tablespoons soy sauce
1 tablespoon Chinese black vinegar
1 teaspoon sesame oil
½ teaspoon chilli oil

Combine the minced pork, Chinese cabbage, Chinese chives and ginger in a bowl. Add the soy sauce, rice wine, sugar and 1 teaspoon salt and mix together very well.

Place a gow gee wrapper flat in the palm of your hand, then place 2 teaspoons of the filling mixture into the centre of the wrapper. With wet fingers, bring the sides together to form a half-moon shape and pinch the seam firmly to seal it in a pleat.

Press one side of the dumplings onto a flat surface to create a flat bottom; this will make them easier to pan-fry.

Heat the oil in a frying pan over medium–high heat. Add the gyoza to the pan in batches and cook for 1–2 minutes on the flat side, without moving, so that the gyoza become brown and crisp on that side. Transfer to a plate. Return the gyoza to the pan in batches, then gradually add 100 ml (3½ fl oz) water to the pan and cover. Steam for 5 minutes. Empty the pan and wipe it dry between batches.

To make the dipping sauce, combine all the ingredients in a small bowl. Serve with the gyoza.

Makes 45

Capsicum muffins with tapenade and mascarpone

1 red capsicum (pepper), cut into large, flattish pieces
250 g (2 cups) plain (all-purpose) flour
3 teaspoons baking powder
75 g (¾ cup) grated Parmesan cheese
125 ml (½ cup) milk
2 eggs, lightly beaten
60 ml (¼ cup) olive oil
1½ tablespoons olive oil, extra
24 fresh basil leaves
75 g (⅓ cup) mascarpone

Tapenade
80 g (½ cup) pitted Kalamata olives
1 garlic clove, chopped
2 anchovies, optional
2 teaspoons drained capers
2 tablespoons olive oil
2 teaspoons lemon juice

Cook the capsicum, skin-side-up, under a hot grill (broiler) until the skin blisters. Allow to cool in a plastic bag. Peel the skin and finely chop the flesh.

Preheat the oven to 180°C (350°F/ Gas 4). Grease 24 non-stick mini muffin holes. Sift the flour and baking powder, add the capsicum and Parmesan, and season. Make a well. Fold in the combined milk, eggs and oil with a metal spoon. Do not overmix — it should be lumpy.

Fill each muffin hole with the mixture. Bake for 15–20 minutes, or until a skewer comes out clean. Cool slightly, then lift out onto a wire rack.

Meanwhile, to make the tapenade, blend the olives, garlic, anchovies and capers in a food processor until finely chopped, then, while the motor is running, add the oil and lemon juice to form a paste. Season with pepper.

Heat the extra oil in a saucepan and fry the basil leaves until they are crisp. Remove and drain on paper towels. While still warm, cut the tops off the muffins. Spread ½ teaspoon of mascarpone on each muffin, then add ½ teaspoon of tapenade. Top with a basil leaf before replacing the 'lids'.

Makes 24

Potato skins

6 large potatoes, unpeeled
oil, for deep-frying

Preheat the oven to 210°C (415°F/ Gas 6–7). Prick each potato with a fork and bake for 1 hour, or until the skins are crisp and the flesh is soft. Turn once during cooking.

Leave the potatoes to cool, then halve them and scoop out the flesh, leaving a thin layer of potato in each shell. Cut each half into 3 wedges.

Fill a deep heavy-based pan one-third full of oil and heat to 190°C (375°F), or until a cube of bread browns in 10 seconds. Cook the potato skins in batches for 2–3 minutes, or until crisp. Drain on paper towels. Sprinkle with salt and pepper.

Makes 36

Turkish pizza

Basic pizza dough
10 g (¼ oz) dried yeast
1 teaspoon caster (superfine) sugar
500 g (4 cups) plain (all-purpose) flour
2 tablespoons olive oil

1 tablespoon olive oil, plus extra
 for brushing
375 g (13 oz) minced (ground) lamb
1 onion, finely chopped
40 g (¼ cup) pine nuts
1 tomato, peeled, seeded and
 chopped
¼ teaspoon ground cinnamon
pinch of allspice
2 teaspoons chopped coriander
 (cilantro), plus extra for serving
2 teaspoons lemon juice
60 g (¼ cup) plain yoghurt

Combine the yeast, sugar and 185 ml
(¾ cup) warm water. Cover and leave
for 10 minutes, or until frothy. If it
hasn't foamed after 10 minutes,
discard and start again.

Sift the flour and ½ teaspoon salt and
make a well. Add the yeast mixture
and oil. Mix with a flat-bladed knife,
using a cutting action, until a dough
forms. Knead for 10 minutes, or until
smooth. Place in an oiled bowl, cover
with plastic wrap and leave for
45 minutes, or until doubled in size.

Heat the oil in a frying pan over
medium heat and cook the mince
for 3 minutes, or until browned. Add
the onion and cook over low heat for
8 minutes, or until soft. Add the pine
nuts, tomato, spices, ¼ teaspoon
cracked pepper and some salt. Cook
for 8 minutes, or until dry. Stir in the
coriander and lemon juice and season.

Preheat the oven to 230°C (450°F/
Gas 8). Punch down the dough, then
knead for 8 minutes, or until elastic.
Roll out into 24 ovals. Spoon some
filling onto each base. Pinch together
the two short sides to form a boat
shape. Brush with oil, and place on a
greased baking tray. Bake for 10 minutes. Serve with yoghurt and coriander.

Makes 24

Preheat the oven to 200°C (400°F/ Gas 6). Cut the red and yellow capsicums into 3 cm (1¼ inch) pieces. Slice the eggplants and zucchini into 1 cm (½ inch) rounds, then thinly slice the onion. Place all the vegetables in a roasting tin with the oil and garlic, then season with salt and cracked black pepper and toss together thoroughly. Roast for 25 minutes, or until cooked.

Spread each half of the focaccia with ½ teaspoon of the pesto and divide the vegetables among them. Place two slices of bocconcini on top of each base, then top with the lid. Toast the focaccias on both sides on a hot chargrill pan until heated through.

Slice each focaccia in half, then wrap a 3 cm (1¼ inch) wide band of double greaseproof paper around the middle of the sandwiches and secure with string. Serve warm.

Makes 24

Mini focaccia with roasted vegetables

2 red capsicums (peppers)
2 yellow capsicums (peppers)
3 slender eggplants (aubergines)
2 large zucchini (courgettes)
1 red onion
80 ml (⅓ cup) extra virgin olive oil
3 garlic cloves, crushed
12 mini focaccias, halved
60 g (¼ cup) ready-made pesto
3 large bocconcini, sliced

Grilled figs in prosciutto

50 g (1¾ oz) unsalted butter
2 tablespoons orange juice
6 small–medium figs
6 long thin slices of prosciutto,
    trimmed of excess fat
24 sage leaves

Think ahead: The figs can be wrapped up to 6 hours in advance and covered in plastic wrap. Cook them just before serving.

Place the butter in a small heavy-based saucepan. Melt over low heat, then cook the butter for 8–10 minutes, or until the froth subsides and the milk solids appear as brown specks on the bottom of the saucepan. Strain the butter into a clean bowl by pouring it through a strainer lined with a clean tea towel or paper towel. Stir the orange juice into the strained butter.

Gently slice the figs lengthways into quarters. Cut each slice of prosciutto into four even strips. Sit a sage leaf on each fig segment, then wrap a piece of prosciutto around the middle with the ends tucked under the bottom of the fig. Arrange the figs, cut-side-up, on a baking tray and brush lightly with the butter mixture.

Move the grill (broiler) tray to its lowest position, then preheat the grill to hot. Place the baking tray of figs on the grill tray and grill (broil) the figs for 1–1½ minutes, or until the prosciutto becomes slightly crispy. Serve hot or at room temperature. If you are serving the figs hot, provide serviettes to avoid burnt fingers.

Makes 24

Prawn and pesto pizza

Pizza dough
7 g (¼ oz) sachet dried yeast
½ teaspoon caster (superfine) sugar
250 g (2 cups) plain (all-purpose) flour
1 tablespoon olive oil

2 tablespoons olive oil
1 teaspoon finely chopped basil
1 garlic clove, crushed
24 cooked medium prawns (shrimp),
    peeled and deveined
60 g (¼ cup) ready-made pesto
24 small basil leaves
24 pine nuts

Combine the yeast, sugar and 185 ml
(¾ cup) warm water, cover and leave
for 10 minutes, or until frothy. If it
hasn't foamed after 10 minutes,
discard and start again.

Sift the flour and ½ teaspoon salt into
a bowl and make a well. Add the yeast
mixture and the oil. Mix with a flat-
bladed knife, using a cutting action,
until a dough forms. Turn onto a
floured surface and knead for
10 minutes, or until smooth. Transfer
to an oiled bowl, cover with plastic
wrap and leave for 45 minutes, or until
doubled in size. Meanwhile, combine
the oil, basil, garlic and prawns in a
non-metallic bowl. Cover with plastic
wrap and refrigerate for 30 minutes.

Preheat the oven to 230°C (450°F/
Gas 8). Punch down the dough, then
knead for 8 minutes, or until elastic.
Divide into 24 balls and roll each ball
into a circle 4 mm (¼ inch) thick and
4.5 cm (1¾ inch) in diameter. Prick the
surfaces with a fork and brush with oil.

Place the bases on a lightly greased
baking tray. Spread ½ teaspoon
of pesto over each base, leaving a
narrow border. Put a prawn, basil leaf
and pine nut on each pizza and bake
for 8–10 minutes.

Makes 24

Pepper and almond bread

2 teaspoons black peppercorns
2 egg whites
90 g (¹⁄₃ cup) caster (superfine) sugar
90 g (³⁄₄ cup) plain (all-purpose) flour
¹⁄₄ teaspoon ground ginger
¹⁄₄ teaspoon ground cinnamon
155 g (1 cup) almonds

Preheat the oven to 180°C (350°F/ Gas 4). Grease an 8 cm x 26 cm (3 inch x 10¹⁄₂ inch) bar tin and line the base and sides with baking paper. Lightly crush the peppercorns with the back of a metal spoon or in a mortar and pestle.

Beat the egg whites and sugar with electric beaters for 4 minutes, or until the mixture turns white and thickens. Sift the flour, ginger and cinnamon and fold in with the almonds and crushed peppercorns.

Spread the mixture into the tin. Bake for 35 minutes, or until lightly browned. Cool in the tin for at least 3 hours, before turning out onto a board. (At this stage, you can wrap the bread in foil and slice the next day.) Using a serrated knife, cut the bread into 3 mm (¹⁄₈ inch) slices. Place the slices in a single layer on baking trays. Bake in a 150°C (300°F/Gas 2) oven for about 25–35 minutes, or until the slices are dry and crisp. Allow to cool completely before serving.

Makes about 70 pieces

Note: To make traditional almond bread, simply remove the peppercorns.

Combine the lamb, curry paste, garlic, ground coriander and half the yoghurt in a non-metallic bowl. Cover and refrigerate for 1–2 hours.

Meanwhile, fill a deep heavy-based saucepan or deep-fryer one-third full of oil and heat to 180°C (350°F), or until a cube of bread browns in 15 seconds. Cook the poppadoms a few at a time for a few seconds each, or until they are puffed and lightly golden. Remove with a slotted spoon and drain on crumpled paper towels.

Lamb korma on mini poppadoms

350 g (12 oz) lamb backstrap or fillet, cut into 1.5 cm (^{5}/$_8$ inch) cubes
2 tablespoons korma curry paste
1 garlic clove, crushed
1 teaspoon ground coriander
125 g (½ cup) thick plain yoghurt
oil, for deep-frying
24 round 4 cm (1½ inch) poppadoms (chilli flavour, if available)
1 tablespoon oil, extra
1½ tablespoons mango chutney
small coriander (cilantro) leaves, to garnish

Heat a wok over high heat, add the extra oil and swirl to coat. Add the marinated lamb and cook in batches, stirring, for 4–5 minutes, or until the lamb is cooked through. Spoon a heaped teaspoon onto each pop-padom and top with ½ teaspoon of the remaining yoghurt, then ¼ tea-spoon of the chutney. Garnish with a coriander leaf and serve immediately.

Makes 24

Think ahead: Lamb korma can be cooked and frozen for up to 2 months, or refrigerated for 2–3 days. Reheat in a saucepan over low heat until warm. Variations: You can make chicken korma instead, by replacing the lamb with 350 g (12 oz) diced chicken tenderloins.

Mini hamburgers

8 burger buns, split in half
400 g (14 oz) minced (ground) beef
25 g (¼ cup) dry breadcrumbs
3 French shallots, very finely chopped
1 tablespoon Dijon mustard
1 tablespoon Worcestershire sauce
80 ml (⅓ cup) tomato sauce
olive oil, for shallow-frying
100 g (3½ oz) thinly sliced Cheddar
   cheese, cut into 24 squares,
   each 3 cm (1¼ inch)
24 baby rocket (arugula) leaves,
   stems removed and torn into
   2.5 cm (1 inch) pieces
12 cornichons (baby gherkins), cut
   into thin slices

Stamp out rounds from the burger buns using a 4 cm (1½ inch) cutter; you should get 24 from the tops and 24 from the bases. If the buns are quite thick, trim them with a serrated knife after you have cut them.

Combine the mince, breadcrumbs, chopped French shallots, mustard, Worcestershire sauce, 1 tablespoon of the tomato sauce and some salt and cracked black pepper in a bowl. Divide the mixture into 24 walnut-sized pieces. With wet hands, shape the pieces into patties.

Heat a large heavy-based frying pan with enough oil to just cover the bottom of the pan and cook the patties over medium heat for about 1 minute on each side, or until browned, then place on a baking tray. Lightly grill (broil) both halves of the mini burger buns. Top each patty with a small slice of cheese and grill for 1 minute, or until the cheese is just starting to melt.

Place the patties on the bottom halves of the burger buns. Top with the rocket, cornichon and remaining tomato sauce. Gently press on the top half of the burger bun and secure with a cocktail stick. Serve warm.

Makes 24

Won ton wrapped prawns

24 raw medium prawns (shrimp)
1 teaspoon cornflour (cornstarch)
24 won ton wrappers
oil, for deep-frying
125 ml (½ cup) sweet chilli sauce
1 tablespoon lime juice

Peel the prawns, leaving the tails intact. Pull out the dark vein from each back, starting at the head end.

Mix the cornflour with 1 teaspoon water in a small bowl. Fold each won ton wrapper in half to form a triangle. Cover them with a tea towel while you are working, to prevent them drying out. Wrap each prawn in a wrapper, leaving the tail exposed. Seal at the end by brushing on a little of the cornflour mixture, then pressing gently. Spread the wrapped prawns on a baking tray, cover with plastic wrap and refrigerate for 20 minutes.

Fill a deep heavy-based saucepan one-third full of oil and heat to 180°C (350°F), or until a cube of bread dropped into the oil browns in 15 seconds. Cook the prawns in batches for 1½ minutes each batch, or until crisp, golden and cooked through. Determine the correct time by cooking one prawn and testing it before continuing. The cooking time may vary depending on the size of the prawns. Remove the prawns from the oil and drain on crumpled paper towels.

Stir the sweet chilli sauce and lime juice together in a small bowl. Serve with the prawns.

Makes 24

Empanadas

2 eggs
40 g (1½ oz) stuffed green olives,
　chopped
95 g (3 oz) ham, finely chopped
30 g (¼ cup) grated Cheddar cheese
3 sheets ready-rolled puff pastry,
　defrosted
1 egg yolk, lightly beaten

Place the eggs in a small saucepan, cover with water and bring to the boil. Boil for 10 minutes, then drain and cool for 5 minutes in cold water. Peel and chop.

Preheat the oven to 220°C (425°F/ Gas 7). Lightly grease two baking trays. Combine the egg, olives, ham and Cheddar in a large bowl.

Cut five 10 cm (4 inch) rounds from each pastry sheet. Place a tablespoon of the filling into the centre of each round, fold the pastry over and crimp the edges to seal.

Place the pastries on the trays, about 2 cm (¾ inch) apart. Brush with the egg yolk and bake in the centre or top half of the oven for 15 minutes, or until well browned and puffed. Swap the trays around after 10 minutes and cover loosely with foil if the empanadas start to brown too much. Serve hot.

Makes 15

One-Bite Nibbles

Pizza wheels

½ small red capsicum (pepper),
  finely chopped
15 g (¼ cup) chopped parsley
2 tablespoons chopped oregano
100 g (3½ oz) finely chopped ham or
  salami
60 g (½ cup) grated Cheddar cheese
60 g (¼ cup) tomato paste (purée)
2 sheets ready-rolled puff pastry,
  defrosted

Preheat the oven to 200°C (400°F/
Gas 6).

Combine the capsicum, parsley,
oregano, ham and cheese in a bowl.

Spread the tomato paste onto each
sheet of pastry, leaving a 2 cm
(¾ inch) border along one side, and
sprinkle the capsicum mixture over
the top. Roll up the pastry to enclose
the filling, leaving the plain edge until
last. Brush the edge lightly with water
and fold over to seal.

Cut each roll into 1 cm (½ inch) rounds
and place onto greased oven trays.
Bake for 20 minutes, or until golden.

Makes 48

Rolled omelette with ocean trout caviar

4 eggs
80 ml (⅓ cup) thick (double/heavy)
  cream
4 tablespoons finely chopped chives
1 tablespoon olive oil
40 g (1½ oz) butter, melted
3 slices white bread
60 g (¼ cup) sour cream
100 g (3½ oz) ocean trout caviar or
  salmon roe
chopped chives, to garnish

Whisk together one egg, 1 tablespoon of the cream and 1 tablespoon of the chopped chives, and season with salt and cracked black pepper. Pour into a 25 cm (10 inch) lightly greased non-stick frying pan and cook over medium heat on one side for 3 minutes, or until just set; the omelettes will be difficult to roll if cooked for too long. Turn out onto a sheet of baking paper. Repeat with the remaining eggs and cream until you have four omelettes. Tightly roll one omelette into a neat roll, then take another omelette and wrap it around the first. Repeat with the remaining omelettes so that you have two rolls. Wrap separately in plastic wrap and refrigerate for 1 hour.

Meanwhile preheat the oven to 180°C (350°F/Gas 4). Combine the oil and butter. Using a 3 cm (1¼ inch) cutter, cut 24 rounds from the bread and brush with the butter and oil mixture. Place on a baking tray and bake for 20–30 minutes, or until crisp and golden. Allow to cool.

Cut each of the cooled omelette rolls into 12 rounds. Spread ½ teaspoon of the sour cream onto each crouton, and sit a round of omelette on top. Top with a teaspoon of salmon roe and garnish with chopped chives.

Makes 24

Herbed pikelets with pear and blue cheese topping

125 g (1 cup) self-raising flour
2 eggs, lightly beaten
125 ml (½ cup) milk
2 tablespoons finely chopped parsley
2 teaspoons finely chopped sage

Pear and blue cheese topping
100 g (3½ oz) Blue Castello or other
  creamy blue cheese
75 g (2½ oz) cream cheese
2 teaspoons brandy
1 large ripe green-skinned pear
30 g (¼ cup) toasted walnuts, finely
  chopped
½ lemon
30 g (1 oz) chives, cut into 3–4 cm
  (1¼–1½ inch) lengths

Sift the flour into a bowl and make a well in the centre. Gradually add the combined eggs and milk, mixing the flour in slowly. When the flour is incorporated, add the parsley and sage and season well. Whisk until a smooth batter forms.

Heat a large non-stick frying pan over medium heat and spray with cooking oil spray. Drop heaped teaspoons of batter into the pan and flatten them to give 5 cm (2 inch) circles. Cook until bubbles appear in the surface of the pikelet, then turn and brown the other side. Lift out to cool on a wire rack.

To make the topping, beat the cheeses and brandy together until smooth. Season with pepper. Cut the pear in half and peel and core one half, then dice it into 5 mm (¼ inch) pieces, leaving the other half untouched. Stir the diced pear and walnuts into the cheese mixture. Core the other half of the pear but do not peel it. Thinly slice the pear length-ways. Cut each slice into 2 cm (¾ inch) triangles with green skin on one side. Squeeze some lemon juice over the cut surfaces to prevent discolouration.

Spread 1 teaspoon of topping on each pikelet. Arrange three pear triangles on top and garnish with chives.

Makes 36

Mexican bites

740 g (1 lb 10 oz) can kidney beans,
  drained
1 teaspoon ground cumin
2 tablespoons olive oil
¼ teaspoon cayenne pepper
1 avocado
1 small garlic clove, crushed
2 tablespoons sour cream
2 tablespoons lime juice
1 vine-ripened tomato, seeded
  and finely chopped
2 tablespoons finely chopped
  coriander (cilantro)
250 g (9 oz) packet round tortilla
  chips

To make the refried beans, put the
kidney beans in a bowl and mash well
with a potato masher, then add the
cumin. Heat 1½ tablespoons of oil in a
large non-stick frying pan and add the
cayenne pepper and mashed kidney
beans. Cook over medium– high heat
for 2–3 minutes, stirring constantly.
Allow to cool, then refrigerate for
about 30 minutes, or until cold.

Scoop the avocado flesh into a food
processor and add the garlic, sour
cream and 1 tablespoon of the lime
juice. Process for a few minutes until
it is a thick creamy paste, then add
salt to taste. Refrigerate.

To make the salsa, mix together the
tomato, coriander and the remaining
olive oil and lime juice in a bowl.
Refrigerate until needed.

To assemble, lay out 36 round tortilla
chips. Put a heaped teaspoon of
refried beans in the centre of each
chip, add a teaspoon of the avocado
cream and lastly half a teaspoon of
tomato salsa.

Makes 36

Think ahead: The bean purée can be
made 3 days in advance. Make the
salsa up to 2 hours beforehand.
Assemble just before serving.

Mini Indian yoghurt bread

1 x 280 g (10 oz) packet Naan
  bread mix
2 spring onions (scallions), finely
  chopped
250 g (1 cup) plain yoghurt
1 tablespoon nigella seeds (kalonji)

Preheat the oven to hot 190°C (375°F/
Gas 5). Empty the bread mix into
a bowl and add the chopped spring
onion. Follow the manufacturer's
instructions to make the dough.

Divide the dough into 4 portions,
then each portion into 6. On a lightly
floured surface, roll each piece out
to a 5 cm (2 inch) round.

Place the rounds on lightly greased
oven trays. Top with a teaspoon of
yoghurt, spread roughly, then sprinkle
with the nigella seeds. Leave for
5 minutes. Bake for 15 minutes, or
until golden brown and crisp.

Makes 24

Smoked salmon bread baskets

250 g (9 oz) smoked salmon
1 loaf white sliced bread
60 ml (¼ cup) olive oil
90 g (⅓ cup) whole-egg mayonnaise
2 teaspoons extra virgin olive oil
1 teaspoon white wine vinegar
1 teaspoon finely chopped dill
3 teaspoons horseradish cream
3 tablespoons salmon roe
dill sprigs, to garnish

Preheat the oven to 180°C (350°F/ Gas 4). Cut the salmon into 2 cm (¾ inch) wide strips. Flatten the bread to 1 mm (¹/₁₆ inch) with a rolling pin, then cut out 24 rounds with a 7 cm (2¾ inch) cutter. Brush both sides of the rounds with oil and push into the holes of two 12-hole flat-based patty tins. Bake for 10 minutes, or until crisp. Cool.

Stir the mayonnaise in a bowl with the extra virgin olive oil, vinegar, dill and horseradish until combined.

Arrange folds of salmon in each cooled bread case and top each with 1 teaspoon of mayonnaise mixture. Spoon ½ teaspoon of salmon roe on top of each, garnish with dill and serve.

Makes 24

Note: The bread cases can be made a day in advance. When completely cold, store in an airtight container. If they soften, you can crisp them on a baking tray in a 180°C (350°F/Gas 4) oven for 5 minutes. Cool before filling.

Asian-flavoured crab tartlets

250 g (2 cups) plain (all-purpose) flour
125 g (4½ oz) chilled butter, chopped
1 egg

Filling
60 ml (¼ cup) lime juice
1 tablespoon fish sauce
1 tablespoon grated palm sugar or
  soft brown sugar
300 g (10½ oz) fresh crab meat,
  shredded and well drained
2 tablespoons chopped coriander
  (cilantro) leaves
1 tablespoon chopped Vietnamese
  mint
1 small red chilli, finely chopped
2 makrut (kaffir) lime leaves, finely
  shredded

Preheat the oven to 200°C (400°F/
Gas 6). Lightly grease 30 mini muffin
holes. Sift the flour into a bowl and rub
the butter in with your fingertips until
the mixture resembles fine breadcrumbs. Make a well in the centre, add
the egg and mix with a flat-bladed
knife, using a cutting action until it
comes together in beads. If the dough
seems too dry, add a little cold water.
Press the dough into a ball on a lightly
floured surface, then wrap it in plastic
wrap and refrigerate for 30 minutes.

Roll out the dough between two
sheets of baking paper to 2 mm
(⅛ inch) thick and cut out 30 rounds
with a 6 cm (2½ inch) cutter. Press
a round into each muffin hole. Prick
the bases with a fork and bake for
6–8 minutes, or until golden. If they
puff up, use a clean tea towel to press
out any air pockets. Cool. Combine
the lime juice, fish sauce and sugar in
a bowl and stir until the sugar is
dissolved. Mix in the rest of the
ingredients, then spoon into the
prepared pastry cases and serve.

Makes 30

Plan ahead: The pastry cases can
be made 2–3 days ahead and kept
in an airtight container. If they go soft,
crisp them in a 170°C (325°F/Gas 3)
oven for 5 minutes.

Cherry tomato and bocconcini tartlets

250 g (2 cups) plain (all-purpose) flour
125 g (4½ oz) chilled butter, chopped
1 egg

Filling
300 g (10½ oz) cherry tomatoes,
    quartered
2 tablespoons olive oil
1 garlic clove, crushed
200 g (7 oz) bocconcini, quartered
80 g (2¾ oz) chopped Kalamata
    olives
1 tablespoon extra virgin olive oil
1 tablespoon torn fresh basil
oil, for deep-frying
30 small fresh basil leaves

Preheat the oven to 200°C (400°F/ Gas 6). Grease 30 mini muffin holes. Sift the flour and rub the butter in with your fingertips until the mixture resembles fine breadcrumbs. Make a well, add the egg and mix with a flat-bladed knife, using a cutting action, until it gathers in beads. Add a little cold water if necessary. Press the dough into a ball, wrap in plastic wrap and chill for 30 minutes.

Roll out the dough between two sheets of baking paper to 2 mm (⅛ inch) thick and cut 30 rounds with a 6 cm (2½ inch) cutter. Press a round into each muffin hole. Prick each base with a fork and bake for 6 minutes, or until dry and golden. If they puff up, use a clean tea towel to press back. Cool.

To make the filling, heat the oven to moderately hot 200°C (400°F/Gas 6). Combine the tomatoes, olive oil and garlic in a roasting tin and bake for 15 minutes, or until golden. Cool, add the bocconcini, olives, extra virgin olive oil and basil, season, and toss. Fill a saucepan one-third full of oil and heat to 180°C (350°F). Deep-fry the basil in batches for 30 seconds, or until crisp. Drain. Spoon the vegetable mixture into the pastry cases and top with a basil leaf.

Makes 30

157

Pork and noodle balls with sweet chilli sauce

Dipping sauce
80 ml (¹⁄₃ cup) sweet chilli sauce
2 teaspoons mirin
2 teaspoons finely chopped fresh
  ginger
125 ml (¹⁄₂ cup) Japanese soy sauce

250 g (9 oz) Hokkien (egg) noodles
300 g (10¹⁄₂ oz) minced (ground) pork
6 spring onions (scallions), finely
  chopped
2 garlic cloves, crushed
20 g (¹⁄₃ cup) finely chopped coriander
  (cilantro) leaves
1 tablespoon fish sauce
2 tablespoons oyster sauce
1¹⁄₂ tablespoons lime juice
peanut oil, for deep-frying

To make the dipping sauce, combine the sweet chilli sauce, mirin, ginger and Japanese soy sauce in a bowl.

Place the noodles in a bowl and cover with boiling water. Soak for 1 minute, or until tender. Drain very well and pat dry with paper towels. Cut the noodles into 5 cm (2 inch) lengths, then transfer to a large bowl. Add the pork, spring onion, garlic, coriander leaves, fish sauce, oyster sauce and lime juice and combine the mixture well using your hands, making sure the pork is evenly distributed throughout the noodles.

Roll a tablespoon of mixture at a time into a ball to make 30 in total, pressing each ball firmly to ensure they stick together during cooking.

Fill a wok or large saucepan one-third full of oil and heat to 170°C (325°F), or until a cube of bread browns in 20 seconds. Deep-fry the pork balls in batches for 2–3 minutes, or until golden and cooked through. Drain on paper towels. Serve hot with the dipping sauce.

Makes 30

Storage: The dipping sauce is best made up to a week in advance to allow the flavours to infuse.

Cucumber cups with Thai beef salad

4 Lebanese (short) cucumbers
oil, for pan-frying
250 g (9 oz) fillet steak
½ red onion, finely chopped
20 mint leaves, finely chopped
1 tablespoon finely chopped
    coriander (cilantro) leaves
1½ tablespoons fish sauce
1½ tablespoons lime juice
1 bird's eye chilli, seeded and finely
    chopped
1 teaspoon grated palm sugar or soft
    brown sugar
small coriander (cilantro) leaves, to
    garnish

Trim each end of the cucumbers but do not peel them. Cut each cucumber into 2 cm (¾ inch) thick slices; you should get 24 pieces. Scoop out the centre of each slice with a melon baller, leaving a shell of flesh.

Heat a large frying pan over high heat and brush lightly with oil. Season the beef with salt and pepper, then place in the pan and cook for 1½–2 minutes each side, depending on the thickness (the beef needs to be rare). Set aside to rest for 5 minutes. Thinly slice the beef across the grain, then slice each piece into 5 mm (¼ inch) wide strips and transfer to a bowl.

Add the onion, mint and coriander to the bowl and mix well. Combine the fish sauce, lime juice, chilli and sugar, stirring until the sugar has dissolved. Pour over the beef mixture and mix well. Fill each cucumber cup with the Thai beef salad and garnish with a whole coriander leaf.

Makes 24

Think ahead: The cups can be prepared a day early. To store them, directly cover the surface with plastic wrap to prevent them from drying out. Store in an airtight container. The meat can also be cooked a day early, but do not slice it until serving.

Deep-fried chicken balls

50 g (1¾ oz) dried rice vermicelli
500 g (1 lb 2 oz) minced (ground)
  chicken
3 garlic cloves, finely chopped
1 tablespoon chopped fresh ginger
1 red chilli, seeded and finely
  chopped
1 egg, lightly beaten
2 spring onions (scallions), finely sliced
20 g (⅓ cup) chopped coriander
  (cilantro) leaves
40 g (⅓ cup) plain (all-purpose) flour
60 g (⅓ cup) finely chopped water
  chestnuts
oil, for deep-frying

Dipping sauce
125 ml (½ cup) sweet chilli sauce
125 ml (½ cup) soy sauce
1 tablespoon Chinese rice wine

Cover the vermicelli with boiling water and soak for 6–7 minutes. Drain, then cut into short lengths.

Combine the mince, garlic, ginger, chilli, egg, spring onion, coriander, flour and water chestnuts in a large bowl. Mix in the vermicelli and season with salt. Refrigerate for 30 minutes. Roll heaped tablespoons of mixture into balls.

Fill a wok or deep saucepan one-third full with oil and heat to 180°C (350°F), or until a cube of bread browns in 15 seconds. Deep-fry the balls in batches for 2 minutes, or until golden brown and cooked through. Drain.

To make the dipping sauce, mix the sweet chilli sauce, soy sauce and rice wine. Serve with the hot chicken balls.

Makes about 30

Spicy chicken goujons

3 chicken breast fillets
plain (all-purpose) flour, for coating
oil, for deep-frying
1/2 teaspoon ground turmeric
1/2 teaspoon ground coriander
1/2 teaspoon ground cumin
1/2 teaspoon chilli powder

Cut the chicken breasts into thin strips and toss in plain flour, shaking off the excess.

Fill a deep heavy-based pan one-third full of oil and heat to 180°C (350°F), or until a cube of bread dropped into the oil browns in 15 seconds. Cook the goujons in batches for 3 minutes, or until golden. Drain on crumpled paper towels and keep warm.

Mix together the turmeric, coriander, cumin, chilli powder and 1 teaspoon salt. Toss the goujons in the mixture, shaking off the excess.

Makes about 30

Scallops with goat's cheese and crispy prosciutto

4 thin slices prosciutto
16 scallops on shells, roe and beards
   removed
2–3 tablespoons extra virgin olive oil
1 tablespoon chopped flat-leaf
   (Italian) parsley
1/2 teaspoon sea salt flakes
100 g (3½ oz) goat's cheese,
   crumbled
2 tablespoons good-quality aged
   balsamic vinegar

Cook the prosciutto under a hot grill (broiler) until crisp, then drain on paper towels and break into small pieces.

Place the scallops on two baking trays. Combine the oil and parsley in a small bowl and season with sea salt and cracked black pepper. Brush the scallops with the oil mixture.

Cook the scallops in batches under a hot grill for 2–3 minutes, or until they are tender.

Top the scallops with the goat's cheese, prosciutto and a drizzle of balsamic vinegar.

Carefully transfer the scallops from the trays to serving plates lined with rock salt — the shells will be very hot. Serve with small cocktail forks to avoid messy fingers.

Makes 16

Mini frittatas

1 kg (2 lb 4 oz) orange sweet potato
1 tablespoon oil
30 g (1 oz) butter
4 leeks, white part only, finely sliced
2 garlic cloves, crushed
250 g (9 oz) feta cheese, crumbled
8 eggs
125 ml (½ cup) cream

Preheat the oven to 180°C (350°F/ Gas 4). Grease or brush a tray of twelve 125 ml (½ cup) muffin holes with oil or melted butter. Cut small rounds of baking paper and place into the base of each hole. Cut the sweet potato into small cubes and boil, steam or microwave until tender. Drain well and set aside.

Heat the oil and butter in a frying pan and cook the leek for 10 minutes, stirring occasionally, or until very soft and lightly golden. Add the garlic and cook for a further 1 minute. Cool, then stir in the feta and sweet potato. Divide the mixture evenly among the muffin holes.

Whisk the eggs and cream together and season with salt and cracked black pepper. Pour the egg mixture into each hole until three-quarters filled, then press the vegetables down gently. Bake for 25–30 minutes, or until golden and set. Leave in the tins for 5 minutes, then ease out with a knife and cool on a wire rack.

Makes 12

Remove the oysters from the shells and pat dry. Wash the shells, replace the oysters and cover with a damp cloth in the fridge.

Place the dill, garlic, parsley, chives, lemon juice and oil in a bowl and season to taste with salt and cracked black pepper. Mix together well, then drizzle a little of the dressing over each oyster.

Garnish with chive bows and serve with tiny cubes of brown bread.

Makes 24

Oysters with lemon herb dressing

24 fresh oysters (see Notes)
1 tablespoon chopped dill
1 garlic clove, crushed
1 tablespoon finely chopped flat-leaf (Italian) parsley
2 teaspoons finely chopped chives
2 tablespoons lemon juice
60 ml ($\frac{1}{4}$ cup) extra virgin olive oil
chive bows, to garnish
brown bread, cubed, to garnish

Notes: Oysters are sold freshly shucked on the half shell, or alive and unshucked. When buying fresh shucked oysters, look for a plump, moist oyster. The flesh should be creamy with a clear liquid (oyster liquor) surrounding it. Oysters should smell like the fresh sea and have no traces of shell particles.
If you prefer to shuck the oysters yourself, look for tightly closed, unbroken shells.
Oysters are often served on a bed of rock salt or crushed ice to help them remain stable and upright, and to keep them cool in summer.

Mushroom ragout tartlets

250 g (2 cups) plain (all-purpose) flour
125 g (4½ oz) chilled butter, chopped
1 egg
50 g (1¾ oz) butter
4 spring onions (scallions), chopped
2 garlic cloves, chopped
150 g (5½ oz) small Swiss brown or
    shiitake mushrooms, thinly sliced
100 g (3½ oz) oyster mushrooms, cut
    into eighths
50 g (1¾ oz) enoki mushrooms,
    trimmed, pulled apart and sliced
    lengthways
3 teaspoons plain (all-purpose) flour
2 tablespoons chicken stock or water
2 tablespoons sake
80 ml (⅓ cup) thick (double/heavy)
    cream
snowpea (mangetout) sprouts, stalks
    removed

Preheat the oven to 200°C (400°F/
Gas 6). Lightly grease 30 mini muffin
holes. Sift the flour and rub the butter
in with your fingertips until the mixture
resembles fine breadcrumbs. Make a
well in the centre, add the egg and
mix with a flat-bladed knife, using a
cutting action until it comes together
in beads. If the dough seems too dry,
add a little cold water. Press the
dough into a ball on a lightly floured
surface, then wrap it in plastic wrap
and refrigerate for 30 minutes.

Roll out the dough between sheets
of baking paper to 2 mm (⅛ inch)
thick. Cut out 30 rounds with a 6 cm
(2½ inch) cutter. Press a round into
each hole. Prick the bases with a
fork and bake for 8 minutes, or until
golden. If they puff up, use a clean
cloth to press back. Cool.

Melt the butter in a frying pan over
medium heat, add the spring onion and
garlic and cook for 1 minute. Add the
mushrooms, stirring, for 3–4 minutes,
or until soft. Add the flour and stir for
another minute. Pour in the stock and
sake and stir until evaporated, then add
the cream and cook for 1 minute, or
until thickened. Season. Spoon into the
prepared pastry cases and top each
one with a snow pea sprout leaf.

Makes 30

173

Roast beef on croûtes

300 g (10½ oz) piece beef eye fillet
80 ml (⅓ cup) olive oil
2 garlic cloves, crushed
2 sprigs thyme, plus extra to garnish
10 slices white bread
1 large garlic clove, peeled, extra

Horseradish cream
80 ml (⅓ cup) thick (double/heavy)
  cream
1 tablespoon horseradish
1 teaspoon lemon juice

Place the beef in a non-metallic bowl, add the combined oil, garlic and thyme and toss to coat. Cover and chill for 3 hours. Preheat the oven to 200°C (400°F/Gas 6).

Cut three rounds from each slice of bread using a 5 cm (2 inch) fluted cutter. Place on a baking tray and bake for 5 minutes each side, then rub the whole garlic clove over each side of the rounds.

To make the horseradish cream, whisk the cream lightly until thickened. Fold in the horseradish and lemon juice, then season with cracked black pepper. Refrigerate until ready to use.

Heat a roasting tin in the oven for 5 minutes. Season the beef on all sides, then place in the hot roasting tin and turn it so that the surface of the meat is sealed. Drizzle with 2 tablespoons of the reserved marinade, then roast for 10 minutes for rare, or until the meat is cooked to your liking. Remove from the oven, cover with foil and rest for 15 minutes before slicing thinly.

Arrange a slice of beef on each croûte, top with ½ teaspoon of the horseradish cream and a small sprig of fresh thyme. Serve immediately.

Makes 30

Salmon cakes with herb mayonnaise

500 g (1 lb 2 oz) salmon fillet, skin
and bones removed, cut into 5 mm
(¼ inch) cubes
3 tablespoons dry breadcrumbs
1 tablespoon lightly beaten egg
½ teaspoon finely grated lime zest
3½ teaspoons lime juice
3 teaspoons dill, chopped
125 g (½ cup) whole-egg mayonnaise
1 garlic clove, crushed
2 tablespoons light olive oil

Place the salmon, breadcrumbs, egg, lime zest, 3 teaspoons lime juice and 2 teaspoons dill in a bowl. Stir until the mixture comes together and the ingredients are evenly distributed. Season well with salt and freshly ground black pepper.

With wet hands, using 2 heaped teaspoons of mixture at a time, shape into 36 small round cakes. Place on a baking tray lined with baking paper. Refrigerate until ready to use.

For the herb mayonnaise, mix the remaining lime juice and dill with the mayonnaise and garlic in a bowl.

Heat the olive oil in a large non-stick frying pan. Cook the salmon cakes in batches over medium heat for 2 minutes each side, or until golden and cooked through. Do not overcook. Drain on paper towels. Top each with a little of the herb mayonnaise and season well. Serve immediately, garnished with lime strips if desired.

Makes 36

Variation: You can also top these with 125 g (½ cup) crème fraîche and 1½ tablespoons salmon roe.

Thai chicken sausage rolls

200 g (7 oz) chicken breast fillet,
    roughly chopped
150 g (5½ oz) mild pancetta,
    chopped
1 garlic clove, crushed
3 spring onions (scallions), chopped
2 tablespoons chopped coriander
    (cilantro)
2 bird's eye chillies, seeded and
    finely chopped
1 teaspoon fish sauce
1 egg
1 teaspoon grated fresh ginger
375 g (13 oz) block frozen puff pastry
1 egg yolk
2 tablespoons sesame seeds
sweet chilli sauce, to serve
coriander (cilantro), to serve

Preheat the oven to 180°C (350°F/
Gas 4). Put the chicken, pancetta,
garlic, spring onion, coriander, chilli,
fish sauce, whole egg and ginger in
a food processor and process until
just combined.

Roll out the pastry to an oblong
30 cm x 40 cm (12 inch x 16 inch).
Cut in half lengthways. Take half the
filling and, using floured hands, roll it
into a long sausage shape and place
along the long edge of one piece of
pastry. Brush the edges with a little
water and fold over, pressing down
to seal. Place the sealed edge
underneath. Repeat with the
remaining pastry and filling.

Using a sharp knife, cut the sausage
rolls into 3 cm (1¼ inch) lengths on
the diagonal; discard the end pieces.
Brush the tops with egg yolk, then
sprinkle with sesame seeds. Bake for
15 minutes, or until golden. Serve
with sweet chilli sauce and garnish
with coriander.

Makes 24

Think ahead: You can make the
sausage rolls a day before the party.
Reheat in a 180°C (350°F/Gas 4)
oven for 10–12 minutes, or until
warmed through.

Blini with caviar

400 ml (14 fl oz) hand-hot milk
3 teaspoons dried yeast
175 g (1 cup and a heaped 1/3 cup)
  plain (all-purpose) flour
50 g (heaped 1/3 cup) buckwheat flour
2 large eggs, separated
70 g (2 1/2 oz) butter
150 ml (5 fl oz) oil
275 g (9 3/4 oz) sour cream
200 g (7 oz) caviar

Fish substitution
  salmon roe, lumpfish roe

Pour half the milk into a jug, sprinkle on the yeast and a tablespoon of the plain flour and whisk well. Leave for 15 minutes until it froths.

Sift the flours and 1/4 teaspoon salt into a large bowl. Add the yeast mixture and the remaining milk. Mix until you have a smooth batter. Cover with a damp tea towel and leave in a warm place until the mixture doubles in size and bubbles, which will take between 1 and 1 1/2 hours.

Whisk the egg whites until stiff peaks form. Stir the egg yolks into the batter, then fold in the egg whites. Cover and leave again to rise for 10 minutes. Pour the mixture into a jug.

Heat one-third of the butter and 2 tablespoons of the oil in a large frying pan and add 1 1/2 tablespoons batter. Cook for 30–60 seconds, or until small bubbles appear in the blini and it begins to turn golden. Flip it over and cook for 1–2 minutes on the other side. Repeat with the remaining batter, adding more butter and oil as needed. Top each blini with sour cream and a little caviar.

Serves 8

Stuffed black olives

36 pitted jumbo black or large
   Kalamata olives (see Note)
100 g (3½ oz) goat's cheese
1 teaspoon capers, drained and finely
   chopped
1 garlic clove, crushed
1 tablespoon chopped flat-leaf
   (Italian) parsley
1½ tablespoons plain (all-purpose)
   flour
2 eggs, lightly beaten
100 g (1 cup) dry breadcrumbs
1 tablespoon finely chopped flat-leaf
   (Italian) parsley, extra
oil, for deep-frying

Carefully cut the olives along the open cavity so they are opened out, but still in one piece.

Mash the goat's cheese, capers, garlic and parsley together in a small bowl, then season. Push an even amount of the mixture into the cavity of the olives, then press them closed.

Put the flour in one small bowl, the egg in another and combine the breadcrumbs and extra parsley in a third. Dip each olive first into the flour, then into the egg and, finally, into the breadcrumbs. Put the crumbed olives on a plate and refrigerate for at least 2 hours.

Fill a deep heavy-based saucepan or deep-fryer one-third full of oil and heat to 180°C (350°F), or until a cube of bread dropped into the oil browns in 15 seconds. Cook the olives in batches for 1–2 minutes, or until golden brown all over; you may need to turn them with tongs or a long-handled metal spoon. Drain on crumpled paper towels and season. Serve warm or at room temperature with lemon wedges.

Makes 36

Note: If you can't find large pitted olives, buy stuffed ones and remove the filling.

Spicy corn puffs

2 corn cobs
3 tablespoons chopped coriander
    (cilantro) leaves
6 spring onions (scallions), finely
    chopped
1 small red chilli, seeded and finely
    chopped
1 large egg
2 teaspoons ground cumin
1/2 teaspoon ground coriander
125 g (1 cup) plain (all-purpose) flour
oil, for deep-frying
sweet chilli sauce, to serve

Cut down the side of the corn with a sharp knife to release the kernels. Roughly chop the kernels, then place them in a large bowl. Holding the cobs over the bowl, scrape down the sides of the cobs with a knife to release any corn juice from the cob into the bowl.

Add the fresh coriander, spring onion, chilli, egg, cumin, ground coriander, 1 teaspoon salt and some cracked black pepper to the bowl and stir well. Add the flour and mix well. The texture of the batter will vary depend-ing on the juiciness of the corn. If the mixture is too dry, add 1 tablespoon water, but no more than that as the batter should be quite dry. Stand for 10 minutes.

Fill a large heavy-based saucepan or deep-fryer one-third full of oil and heat to 180°C (350°F), or until a cube of bread dropped in the oil browns in 15 seconds. Drop slightly heaped teaspoons of the corn batter into the oil and cook for about 1 1/2 minutes, or until puffed and golden. Drain on crumpled paper towels and serve immediately with a bowl of the sweet chilli sauce to dip the puffs into.

Makes about 36

Note: The corn puffs should be prepared just before serving.

Cauliflower fritters

600 g (1 lb 5 oz) cauliflower
55 g (1/2 cup) besan (chickpea flour)
2 teaspoons ground cumin
1 teaspoon ground coriander
1 teaspoon ground turmeric
pinch cayenne pepper
1 egg, lightly beaten
1 egg yolk
oil, for deep-frying

Cut the cauliflower into bite-sized florets. Sift the flour and spices into a bowl, then stir in 1/2 teaspoon salt.

Lightly whisk the beaten egg, egg yolk and 60 ml (1/4 cup) water in a jug. Make a well in the centre of the dry ingredients and pour in the egg mixture, whisking until smooth. Stand for 30 minutes.

Fill a deep saucepan one-third full of oil and heat to 180°C (350°F), or until a cube of bread dropped into the oil browns in 15 seconds. Dip the florets into the batter, allowing the excess to drain into the bowl. Deep-fry in batches for 3–4 minutes per batch, or until puffed and browned. Drain, sprinkle with salt and extra cayenne, if desired, and serve hot.

Serves 4–6

Preheat the oven to 200°C (400°F/ Gas 6). Lightly grease 30 mini muffin holes. Sift the flour into a large bowl and rub the butter in with your fingertips until the mixture resembles fine breadcrumbs. Make a well in the centre, add the egg and mix with a flat-bladed knife, using a cutting action until it comes together in beads. If the dough seems too dry, add a little cold water. Press the dough into a ball on a lightly floured surface, then wrap it in plastic wrap and refrigerate for 30 minutes.

Creamed egg with roe tartlets

Basic pastry cases
250 g (2 cups) plain (all-purpose) flour
125 g (4½ oz) chilled butter, chopped
1 egg

4 eggs and 4 egg yolks
75 g (2½ oz) unsalted butter
4 tablespoons roe

Roll out the dough between two sheets of baking paper to 2 mm (⅛ inch) thick and cut out 30 rounds with a 6 cm (2½ inch) cutter. Press a round into each muffin hole. Prick the bases with a fork and bake for 6–8 minutes, or until dry and golden. If they puff up, use a clean tea towel to press out the air. Cool. Lightly beat the eggs and egg yolks together. Melt the butter over very low heat, then add the eggs and whisk slowly and constantly for 5–6 minutes, or until the mixture is thick and creamy but the eggs are not scrambled. Remove from the heat straight away and season to taste. Fill each pastry case with 1 teaspoon of the creamed egg mixture, then top with ½ teaspoon of roe before serving.

Makes 30

189

Spicy fish cakes

2 small dried red chillies
14 pieces of banana leaf measuring
  16 x 12 cm (6½ x 5 inches)
  (foil can be used instead)
450 g (1 lb) grouper fillets, skinned
  and cut into chunks
1 stem of lemon grass, cut into three
1 small onion, cut in half
1 large garlic clove, peeled
generous pinch of ground turmeric
1 teaspoon grated palm sugar or soft
  brown sugar
1 teaspoon ground coriander
1 teaspoon shrimp paste
1 tablespoon candlenuts or unsalted
  macadamias or peanuts
1 tablespoon chopped mint
1 tablespoon chopped coriander
  (cilantro) leaves
60 ml (¼ cup) coconut milk

Fish substitution
  hapuka, blue warehou, halibut,
  haddock, snapper

Remove stalks and soak the chillies in boiling water. Soak 14 cocktail sticks in cold water. If you are using fresh banana leaves, blanch them in boiling water for a minute, then drain and refresh in cold water.

Put the fish in a food processor and blend to a thick purée. Scoop into a bowl. Drain the chillies and put in the processor along with the rest of the ingredients and a pinch of salt. Blend to a paste. Add the paste to the fish and mix well.

Drain the cocktail sticks. Put about 2 tablespoons of mixture in the middle of each piece of banana leaf. Fold the shorter sides of the rectangle into the middle so they overlap. Tuck the two protruding ends underneath to make a small package. Secure the two ends with a cocktail stick. Put the parcels smooth-side down on a barbecue hotplate or heated frying pan and cook for 5 minutes, or until the banana leaf has lightly browned and the parcels are hot in the middle. Unwrap before eating.

Makes 14

Prawn toasts

Dipping sauce
125 ml (1/2 cup) tomato sauce
2 garlic cloves, crushed
2 small red chillies, seeded and finely
    chopped
2 tablespoons hoisin sauce
2 teaspoons Worcestershire sauce

350 g (12 oz) raw medium prawns
    (shrimp)
1 garlic clove
75 g (2 1/2 oz) canned water chestnuts,
    drained
1 tablespoon chopped coriander
    (cilantro)
2 cm x 2 cm (3/4 inch x 3/4 inch) piece
    fresh ginger, roughly chopped
2 eggs, separated
1/4 teaspoon white pepper
12 slices white bread, crusts removed
155 g (1 cup) sesame seeds
oil, for deep-frying

To make the dipping sauce, combine all the ingredients in a small bowl.

Peel the prawns and gently pull out the dark vein from each prawn back, starting at the head end. Put the prawns in a food processor with the garlic, water chestnuts, coriander, ginger, egg whites, pepper and 1/4 teaspoon salt and process for 20–30 seconds, or until smooth.

Brush the top of each slice of bread with lightly beaten egg yolk, then spread evenly with the prawn mixture. Sprinkle generously with sesame seeds. Cut each slice of bread into three even strips.

Fill a large heavy-based saucepan one-third full of oil and heat to 180°C (350°F), or until a cube of bread browns in 15 seconds. Deep-fry the toasts in batches for 10–15 seconds, or until golden and crisp. Start with the prawn mixture face down, then turn halfway. Remove the toasts from the oil with tongs or a slotted spoon and drain on crumpled paper towels. Serve with the dipping sauce.

Makes 36

Salt-and-pepper squid

1 kg (2 lb 4 oz) squid tubes, halved
  lengthways
250 ml (1 cup) lemon juice
250 g (2 cups) cornflour (cornstarch)
1½ tablespoons salt
1 tablespoon ground white pepper
2 teaspoons caster (superfine) sugar
4 egg whites, lightly beaten
oil, for deep-frying
lemon wedges, for serving
coriander (cilantro) leaves, for garnish

Open out the squid tubes, wash and pat dry. Lay on a chopping board with the inside facing upwards. Score a fine diamond pattern on the squid, being careful not to cut all the way through. Cut into pieces about 5 x 3 cm (2 x 1¼ inches). Place in a flat non-metallic dish and pour the lemon juice over the top. Cover and refrigerate for 15 minutes. Drain and pat dry.

Combine the cornflour, salt, white pepper and sugar in a bowl. Dip the squid into the egg white and then into the flour mixture, shaking off any excess.

Fill a deep-fat fryer or large saucepan one-third full of oil and heat to 180°C (350°F), or until a small cube of white bread dropped into the oil turns golden brown in 15 seconds. Cook batches of the squid for 1–2 minutes, or until the flesh turns white and curls. Drain on crumpled paper towels. Serve with lemon wedges and garnish with coriander.

Serves 6

Salt cod fritters

500 g (1 lb 2 oz) salt cod
1 large potato (200 g/7 oz), unpeeled
2 tablespoons milk
60 ml (¼ cup) olive oil
1 small onion, finely chopped
2 garlic cloves, crushed
30 g (¼ cup) self-raising flour
2 eggs, separated
1 tablespoon finely chopped flat-leaf
  (Italian) parsley
oil, for deep-frying

Soak the cod in cold water for 24 hours, changing the water at least three times. Boil the potato for 20 minutes, or until soft. Drain. When cool enough to handle, peel and mash with the milk and 2 tablespoons of the olive oil. Drain the cod, cut into pieces and place in a saucepan. Cover with cold water, bring to the boil over high heat, then simmer for 10 minutes, or until soft. Drain. When cool enough to handle, remove the skin and any bones. Mash with a fork until flaky. (You should have 200 g/7 oz of flesh.)

Heat the remaining olive oil in a frying pan. Cook the onion over medium heat for 5 minutes, or until softened and browning. Add the garlic and cook for 1 minute. Remove from the heat.

Combine the potato, cod, onion mixture, flour, egg yolks and parsley, and season with cracked black pepper. Whisk the egg whites until stiff then fold into the mixture. Fill a large heavy-based saucepan one-third full with oil and heat to 190°C (375°F), or until a cube of bread browns in 10 seconds. Drop level tablespoons of the mixture into the oil and cook for 2 minutes, or until puffed and golden. Drain on crumpled paper towels and serve.

Makes 28

Caramelized onion tartlets with feta and thyme

1½ sheets ready-rolled shortcrust
  pastry
30 g (1 oz) unsalted butter
750 g (1 lb 10 oz) thinly sliced
  red onion
1½ tablespoons soft brown sugar
1½ tablespoons balsamic vinegar
1 teaspoon chopped thyme
100 g (3½ oz) feta cheese
thyme sprigs, garnish

Preheat the oven to 180°C (350°F/
Gas 4). Using a 5 cm (2 inch) round
cutter, cut out 24 circles of pastry.
Place in lightly greased patty tins and
bake for 15 minutes, or until golden.

Meanwhile, melt the butter in a large
frying pan. Add the red onion and
cook over low heat for 35–40 minutes,
or until soft and golden. Add the
brown sugar, balsamic vinegar and
thyme. Season. Cook for another
10 minutes, then spoon into the
pastry shells.

Crumble the feta over the tartlets and
place under a hot grill (broiler) for
30 seconds, or until the cheese melts
slightly. Top with sprigs of thyme and
serve immediately.

Makes 24

Sesame and wasabi-crusted tuna cubes

Ginger and soy dipping sauce
2 cm x 2 cm (³/₄ inch x ³/₄ inch) piece
   fresh ginger, cut into julienne strips
2 tablespoons Japanese soy sauce
2 tablespoons mirin
1 teaspoon wasabi paste
¼ teaspoon sesame oil

Tuna cubes
600 g (1 lb 5 oz) fresh tuna steaks
1 teaspoon wasabi powder
50 g (⅓ cup) black sesame seeds
60 ml (¼ cup) oil

To make the dipping sauce, combine the ginger, Japanese soy sauce, mirin, wasabi paste and sesame oil.

Cut the tuna into 2 cm (³/₄ inch) cubes using a very sharp knife. Toss with the combined wasabi powder and black sesame seeds until evenly coated.

Heat a wok over high heat, add half the oil and swirl to coat. Add half the tuna and cook, tossing gently, for 1–2 minutes, or until lightly golden on the outside but still pink in the middle. Drain on crumpled paper towels and repeat with the remaining oil and tuna. Arrange on a platter with dipping sauce in the centre and serve with toothpicks so that your guests can pick up the cubes.

Makes about 40

Think ahead: The dipping sauce will keep in the refrigerator for up to 1 week, but the tuna is best if cooked no more than 3 hours in advance.Variation: Try a chilli and lime dipping sauce instead of the ginger and soy one above. Dissolve 2 tablespoons grated palm sugar or soft brown sugar in 2 table-spoons lime juice. Add 1 tablespoon fish sauce and 1 seeded and chopped red bird's eye chilli. Mix together well. This sauce will keep in the refrigerator for 2–3 days.

Tahini and chilli palmiers

135 g (½ cup) tahini
1 red chilli, seeded and finely
   chopped
½ teaspoon paprika
2 sheets ready-rolled frozen puff
   pastry, defrosted

Preheat the oven to 200°C (400°F/ Gas 6). Combine the tahini, chilli and paprika. Spread half the mixture over each sheet of pastry (to the edges).

Fold the pastry from opposite sides until the folds meet in the middle. Then fold one side over the other to resemble a closed book. Refrigerate for 5 minutes to firm.

Cut into 1.5 cm (⅝ inch) slices and place on baking trays lined with baking paper, leaving room for spreading.

Bake for 8 minutes, then turn over and bake for 2 minutes, or until golden brown.

Makes 36

Money bags

1 tablespoon peanut oil
4 red Asian shallots, finely chopped
2 garlic cloves, crushed
1 tablespoon grated fresh ginger
150 g (5½ oz) minced (ground) chicken
150 g (5½ oz) minced (ground) pork
40 g (¼ cup) roasted peanuts, chopped
3 tablespoons finely chopped
   coriander (cilantro) leaves
3 teaspoons fish sauce
2 teaspoons soy sauce
2 teaspoons lime juice
2 teaspoons grated palm sugar or
   soft brown sugar
30 won ton wrappers
oil, for deep-frying
garlic chives, for tying

Dipping sauce
2 teaspoons sugar
125 ml (½ cup) vinegar
2 small red chillies, seeded and chopped

Heat the oil in a frying pan over medium heat. Add the shallots, garlic and ginger and cook for 1–2 minutes. Add the minced chicken and pork and cook for 4 minutes, breaking up any lumps with a wooden spoon. Stir in the peanuts, coriander, fish sauce, soy sauce, lime juice and sugar and cook, stirring, for 1–2 minutes, or until mixed and reduced. Cool.

Form your thumb and index finger into a circle, and place a won ton wrapper on top. Place 2 teaspoons of the cooled mixture in the centre, then lightly brush the edges with water. Push the mixture down firmly with your free hand, tightening the circle of your thumb and index finger at the same time, encasing the mixture in the wrapper and forming a 'bag'. Trim.

Fill a deep heavy-based saucepan or deep-fryer one-third full of oil and heat to 190°C (375°F), or until a cube of bread browns in 10 seconds. Cook in batches for 30–60 seconds, or until golden. Drain. Tie the 'neck' of the money bags with the chives.

To make the dipping sauce, dissolve the sugar and 1 teaspoon salt in the vinegar. Add the chilli and mix. Serve with the dipping sauce.

Makes 30

Mini crab cakes with coriander paste

1 tablespoon butter
4 spring onions (scallions), sliced
1 egg
2 tablespoons sour cream
350 g (12 oz) fresh white crab meat,
    excess liquid squeezed out
1 small yellow capsicum (pepper),
    finely diced
2 teaspoons chopped thyme
200 g (2½ cups) fresh white
    breadcrumbs
olive oil, for shallow-frying

Coriander paste
1 garlic clove
1 green chilli, seeded
½ teaspoon ground cumin
¼ teaspoon sugar
25 g (¾ cup) coriander (cilantro) leaves
10 g (½ cup) mint
1 tablespoon lemon juice
25 ml (1 fl oz) coconut cream
½ avocado

Line a tray with baking paper. Melt the butter in a frying pan over low heat. When it begins to foam, add the spring onion and cook for 2 minutes, or until softened. Remove from the heat and cool.

Mix the egg and sour cream until just smooth. Add the spring onion, crab, capsicum, thyme and 40 g (½ cup) of the breadcrumbs, season and mix. Shape the mixture into flat rounds, using 1 level tablespoon for each. Place on the tray and refrigerate for 30 minutes.

Meanwhile, to make the coriander paste, process the garlic, chilli, cumin, sugar, herbs, lemon juice and ¼ tea-spoon salt in a food processor until a fine paste forms. Add the coconut cream and continue to blend until smooth. Add the avocado and, using the pulse action, process until just smooth. Transfer to a bowl, cover with plastic wrap and chill. Using your hands, coat the crab cakes in the remaining breadcrumbs. Heat enough olive oil in a non-stick frying pan to just coat the bottom. Cook in batches for 2–3 minutes each side, or until golden. Drain and serve warm with ½ teaspoon of coriander paste on each.

Makes 24

Oysters with ginger and lime

12 oysters, shucked, in their shells
½ teaspoon finely grated fresh ginger
zest and juice of 2 limes
2 teaspoons Thai fish sauce
1 tablespoon chopped coriander
  (cilantro) leaves
2 teaspoons sugar
lime wedges, for serving

Nestle the opened oysters on a bed
of crushed ice or rock salt on a large
platter (this will keep them steady).

Mix the ginger, lime zest and juice,
fish sauce, coriander and sugar
together. Drizzle a little of the sauce
into each oyster shell and serve with
lime wedges.

Serves 2

Udon noodle sushi rolls

300 g (10½ oz) flat udon or
    soba noodles
6 sheets roasted nori
50 g (1¾ oz) pickled daikon, cut
    into long, thin strips
3 tablespoons drained red pickled
    ginger shreds
ponzu sauce, for dipping (see Note)

Cook the udon or soba noodles
according to the packet instructions
or until tender. Rinse under cold water
and pat dry.

Working on a flat surface, lie one
sheet of nori on a sushi mat. Top with
one-sixth of the noodles along the
bottom half of the nori, then arrange
the daikon and the pickled ginger
along the centre of the noodles. Roll
the nori up firmly to enclose the filling.
Cut the roll in half and then each half
into three equal pieces. Repeat with
the remaining ingredients. Serve with
the ponzu sauce.

Makes 36 pieces

Note: Ponzu is a Japanese dipping
sauce made from rice vinegar, soy,
mirin and dashi.

211

Bigger Bites

Prawn skewers with coconut sambal

80 ml (⅓ cup) coconut cream
60 ml (¼ cup) lime juice
2 tablespoons soy sauce
1 tablespoon grated lime zest
2 teaspoons chopped red chilli
1 teaspoon grated palm sugar
  or soft brown sugar
½ teaspoon shrimp paste
4 garlic cloves, crushed
32 raw medium prawns (shrimp), peeled
  and deveined, with tails intact
2 teaspoons oil
1 tablespoon chopped coriander
  (cilantro)
mango chutney

Coconut sambal
25 g (¼ cup) desiccated coconut
40 g (¼ cup) sesame seeds
½ teaspoon dried garlic flakes
¼ teaspoon ground coriander
¼ teaspoon ground cumin
40 g (¼ cup) roasted unsalted
  peanuts, roughly chopped

Soak eight bamboo skewers in water for 30 minutes. Combine the coconut cream, lime juice, soy sauce, lime zest, chilli, sugar, shrimp paste and garlic and mix until the sugar dissolves.

Thread four prawns on each skewer. Place on a non-metallic plate and pour the marinade over them and refrigerate, covered, for 1 hour.

To make the sambal, toast the coconut in a dry frying pan for 1–2 minutes, or until golden, then add the sesame seeds, garlic flakes, spices and ½ teaspoon salt and cook for about 30 seconds. Remove from the heat and stir in the peanuts. Spoon into a small serving bowl.

Heat a chargrill pan or barbecue hotplate to high and brush with a little oil. Cook the prawns on both sides for 2–3 minutes, or until pink and cooked. Place on a platter and sprinkle with coriander. Serve with the sambal and chutney.

Serves 4

Drumsticks in tomato and mango chutney

8 chicken drumsticks, scored
1 tablespoon mustard powder
2 tablespoons tomato sauce
1 tablespoon sweet mango chutney
1 teaspoon Worcestershire sauce
1 tablespoon Dijon mustard
30 g (¼ cup) raisins
1 tablespoon oil

Toss the chicken in the mustard powder and season with salt and ground black pepper. Combine the tomato sauce, mango chutney, Worcestershire sauce, mustard, raisins and oil. Spoon over the chicken and toss well. Marinate for at least 2 hours, turning once.

Cook the chicken on a hot, lightly oiled barbecue flat plate for about 20 minutes, or until cooked through.

Serves 4

Grilled haloumi salad

1½ tablespoons lemon juice
2 tablespoons finely chopped mint
    leaves
125 ml (½ cup) olive oil
2 garlic cloves
8 slices ciabatta bread
300 g (10½ oz) haloumi cheese,
    cut into 5 mm (½ inch) slices
3 ripe tomatoes
150 g (5½ oz) rocket (arugula) leaves
2 tablespoons pine nuts, toasted

Whisk the lemon juice, mint, 60 ml (¼ cup) of olive oil and 1 clove of crushed garlic together, and season with salt and pepper.

Brush both sides of each slice of bread with 1 tablespoon of olive oil and season well. Brush the haloumi with 1 tablespoon of olive oil. Cut the tomatoes into 1 cm (½ inch) rounds, brush with 1 tablespoon olive oil and season well.

Preheat a barbecue to medium direct heat and chargrill the bread for 1 minute on each side, or until it is golden and marked. Rub each piece on both sides with the remaining clove of garlic. Wrap the toast in foil and keep it warm on the side of the barbecue. Chargrill the haloumi and tomato for 3–5 minutes on each side, or until they are browned, then drizzle with 1 tablespoon of the mint and lemon dressing.

Put the rocket and pine nuts in a large bowl, add the remaining dressing and toss gently until the salad is coated with the dressing. Pile some onto a piece of the garlic toast, arrange some grilled haloumi and tomato across the top and serve it warm.

Serves 4

Spicy buffalo wings with ranch dressing

12 large chicken wings
2 teaspoons garlic salt
2 teaspoons onion powder
oil, for deep-frying
125 ml (½ cup) tomato sauce
2 tablespoons Worcestershire sauce
50 g (1¾ oz) butter, melted
Tabasco sauce, to taste

Ranch dressing
1 small garlic clove, crushed
185 g (¾ cup) mayonnaise
125 ml (½ cup) buttermilk
2 tablespoons finely chopped
   flat-leaf (Italian) parsley
1 tablespoon finely chopped chives
1½ teaspoons lemon juice
1½ teaspoons Dijon mustard
1 teaspoon onion powder

Pat the wings dry with paper towels, remove and discard the tip of each wing, then cut them in half at the joint. Combine the garlic salt, onion powder and 2 teaspoons of ground black pepper, and rub the spice mixture into each chicken piece.

Deep-fry the chicken in batches for 2–3 minutes without letting it brown, then remove from the oil and drain on crumpled paper towels. When the chicken has cooled a little, put it in a non-metallic bowl with the combined tomato sauce, Worcestershire sauce, butter and Tabasco, and toss so that all of the pieces are well coated in the marinade. Cover and refrigerate for at least 2 hours, or overnight.

To make the ranch dressing, mash the garlic and ¼ teaspoon salt to a paste then add the mayonnaise, buttermilk, parsley, chives, lemon juice, mustard and onion powder, and whisk it all together. Season well, cover and chill for at least 1 hour before serving.

Preheat a barbecue to medium direct heat. Cook the chicken for 6–8 minutes on each side, or until it is caramelized and sticky, turning and basting with the marinade as it cooks. Serve hot with the ranch dressing.

Serves 4

Barbecued honey chicken wings

12 chicken wings
4 tablespoons soy sauce
3 tablespoons sherry
3 tablespoons oil
1 garlic clove, crushed
3 tablespoons honey

Rinse the chicken wings, then give them a thorough pat with paper towels to dry them. Tuck the wing tips into the underside.

Put the chicken wings in a shallow non-metallic dish. Whisk together the soy sauce, sherry, oil and garlic, then pour all over the chicken wings, lightly tossing for good measure. Cover with plastic wrap, then leave in the fridge for 2 hours to give the chicken a chance to take up some of the marinade — it will help if you turn the wings occasionally.

The honey needs to be heated enough for it to become brushing consistency — either use the microwave or warm it gently in a small saucepan.

Lightly grease a barbecue or chargrill pan (griddle) and heat it up. Lift the chicken out of the marinade and add it to the hot pan. Cook the chicken wings until tender and cooked through, turning occasionally — this should take about 12 minutes. Now brush the wings with the warmed honey and cook for 2 minutes more.

Serves 4

Cut the chicken into strips. First, dust the chicken strips with the flour, then dip them in the egg and, finally, coat them in the combined nuts and breadcrumbs. Refrigerate for at least 30 minutes to firm up.

Fill a large heavy-based saucepan or deep-fryer one-third full of oil and heat to 180°C (350°F), or until a cube of bread dropped in the oil browns in 15 seconds. Cook the chicken in batches for 2–3 minutes, or until golden brown all over, taking care not to burn the nuts. Drain on crumpled paper towels. Serve warm.

Macadamia-crusted chicken strips

12 chicken tenderloins (700 g/
   1 lb 9 oz), larger ones cut in half
seasoned plain (all-purpose) flour,
   to dust
2 eggs, lightly beaten
250 g (9 oz) macadamia nuts, finely
   chopped
160 g (2 cups) fresh breadcrumbs
oil, to deep-fry

Makes 24

Variations: The chicken strips are very tasty served with sweet chilli sauce or a mango salsa. Try making your own salsa by combining one small, finely diced mango, 2 tablespoons finely diced red onion, 2 tablespoons roughly chopped, fresh coriander (cilantro) leaves, one fresh green chilli, seeded and finely chopped, and 1 tablespoon of lime juice. Season to taste. Try a different coating using almonds or peanuts.

Turkish bread with herbed zucchini

½ large loaf Turkish bread
1 tablespoon sesame seeds
125 ml (½ cup) vegetable oil

Herbed zucchini
1 tablespoon olive oil
2 garlic cloves, finely chopped
4 x 100 g (3½ oz) small zucchini
   (courgettes), roughly chopped
1 large carrot, thinly sliced
2 tablespoons chopped flat-leaf
   (Italian) parsley
2 tablespoons chopped mint
2 teaspoons lemon juice
½ teaspoon ground cumin

Split the bread horizontally through the middle and open it out. Cut the bread into 3 cm (1¼ inch) squares; you should end up with 48 squares.

Toast the sesame seeds in a large dry non-stick frying pan over low heat for 2–3 minutes, or until golden. Remove from the pan. Heat the vegetable oil in the same pan and cook the bread in batches for 1–2 minutes each side, or until crisp and golden. Drain on paper towels.

Heat the olive oil in a saucepan over medium heat and cook the garlic for 1 minute. Add the zucchini and carrot and cook over medium heat for 2 minutes. Season with salt and pepper. Add 1 tablespoon water, cover and simmer over low heat for 15 minutes, or until the vegetables are soft. Spoon into a bowl and mash roughly with a potato masher. Add the parsley, mint, lemon juice and cumin. Season to taste.

Spoon 2 teaspoons of the zucchini mixture over each square of bread and scatter with sesame seeds. Serve warm or at room temperature.

Makes 48

Think ahead: The herbed zucchini can be prepared up to 2 days in advance. Reheat just before serving.

Put the lamb in a large, non-metallic bowl. Add the combined olive oil, lemon juice, garlic, pepper, mustard and oregano. Toss well, cover and refrigerate for at least 3 hours.

Soak 12 wooden skewers in water to prevent scorching. Drain the lamb, reserving the marinade. Thread the lamb onto the skewers and cook on a hot, lightly oiled barbecue grill or flat plate until well browned, brushing with the marinade occasionally.

Skewered lamb with chilli aïoli

1.5 kg (3 lb 5 oz) leg of lamb,
  boned and cubed
125 ml (½ cup) olive oil
125 ml (½ cup) lemon juice
2 garlic cloves, crushed
1 teaspoon cracked black pepper
1 tablespoon Dijon mustard
1 tablespoon chopped oregano

Chilli aïoli
2–3 small red chillies, seeded
3 garlic cloves
½ teaspoon ground black pepper
3 egg yolks
2 tablespoons lemon juice
200 ml (7 fl oz) olive oil

To make the chilli aïoli, chop the chillies and garlic for 30 seconds in a food processor. Add the pepper, egg yolks and 2 teaspoons of lemon juice. With the motor running, slowly pour in the oil in a fine stream. Increase the flow as the aïoli thickens. Add the remaining lemon juice and season to taste. Serve with the skewered lamb.

Makes 12 skewers

Mushroom and eggplant skewers with tomato sauce

12 long rosemary sprigs
18 Swiss brown mushrooms, halved
1 small eggplant (aubergine), cubed
60 ml (¼ cup) olive oil
2 tablespoons balsamic vinegar
2 garlic cloves, crushed
1 teaspoon sugar

Tomato sauce
5 tomatoes
1 tablespoon olive oil
1 small onion, finely chopped
1 garlic clove, crushed
1 tablespoon tomato paste (purée)
2 teaspoons sugar
2 teaspoons balsamic vinegar
1 tablespoon chopped flat-leaf
   (Italian) parsley

Remove the leaves from the lower part of the rosemary sprigs. Reserve 1 tablespoon of the leaves. Put the mushrooms and eggplant in a large non-metallic bowl. Pour on the combined oil, vinegar, garlic and sugar and toss. Marinate for about 15 minutes.

To make the tomato sauce, score a cross in the base of each tomato. Put in a bowl of boiling water for 30 seconds, then plunge into cold water. Peel the skin away from the cross. Cut in half and scoop out the seeds with a teaspoon. Dice the flesh.

Heat the oil in a saucepan. Cook the onion and garlic over medium heat for 2–3 minutes, or until soft. Reduce the heat, add the tomato, tomato paste, sugar, vinegar and parsley and simmer for 10 minutes, or until thick.

Carefully thread alternating mushroom halves and eggplant cubes onto the rosemary sprigs. Cook on a hot, lightly oiled barbecue grill or flat plate for 7–8 minutes, or until the eggplant is tender, turning occasionally. Serve with the sauce.

Serves 4

Burgundy beef pies

Filling
2 tablespoons olive oil
500 g (1 lb 2 oz) diced lean beef
  (topside)
1 onion, finely chopped
50 g (1¾ oz) pancetta, finely chopped
2 garlic cloves, crushed
1 tablespoon tomato paste (purée)
250 ml (1 cup) red wine
125 ml (½ cup) beef stock
1 teaspoon dried Italian herbs
125 g (½ cup) puréed tomatoes

750 g (1 lb 10 oz) ready-made
  shortcrust pastry
1 egg, lightly beaten

Heat half the oil in a large saucepan and cook the beef in batches over high heat for 5 minutes, or until browned. Remove the meat and set aside. Add the remaining oil and cook the onion, pancetta and garlic for 3–4 minutes, or until soft. Return the meat to the pan, stir in the rest of the ingredients, cover and simmer for 50–60 minutes, or until the meat is tender. Remove the lid and cook for a further 30 minutes, or until the sauce is reduced. Allow to cool.

Preheat the oven to 180°C (350°F/ Gas 4) and put a baking tray in the oven. Grease 24 mini muffin holes. Roll the pastry thinly and cut out 24 rounds with a 7 cm (2¾ inch) cutter. Repeat with a 5.5 cm (2¼ inch) cutter. Put one of the larger rounds in each muffin hole and fill with the cooled filling. Dampen the edges of the small rounds and place them on top of the filling to seal the pies. Brush with egg. Put the tin on the hot baking tray and cook for 25 minutes, or until golden. Cool slightly, then remove from the tin.

Makes 24

Bruschetta with mushrooms and mustard crème fraîche

5 small field mushrooms (about
    300 g/10½ oz), quartered
1 red onion, halved and thinly sliced
170 ml (⅔ cup) olive oil
3 garlic cloves, crushed
1½ tablespoons chopped oregano
    leaves
60 g (¼ cup) crème fraîche
1 teaspoon Dijon mustard
1 loaf ciabatta bread
60 ml (¼ cup) olive oil, extra
1 large garlic clove, extra, peeled
    and halved
small oregano leaves
150 g (6 handfuls) mixed lettuce
    leaves
2 tablespoons extra virgin olive oil
1 tablespoon lemon juice

Put the mushrooms and onion in separate bowls and season each well. Whisk together the oil, garlic and oregano and pour two-thirds of the mixture over the mushrooms and the rest over the onion. Toss until well coated in the marinade, then cover and refrigerate for 30 minutes. Mix the crème fraîche and mustard together, then refrigerate it until needed.

Heat a barbecue to medium direct heat. Cut the bread into twelve 1 cm (½ inch) thick slices and brush both sides of each slice with the extra oil. Toast the bread on the chargrill plate for 1–2 minutes on each side or until golden and lightly charred, then rub one side of each slice with the cut side of the garlic clove. Cook the onion on the flat plate, tossing gently, for 2–3 minutes or until soft and golden. Cook the mushrooms on the flat plate for 2 minutes each side or until cooked through, then toss the onion and mushrooms together.

Arrange the mushrooms and onion on the garlic side of the bread slices and top with a teaspoon of mustard crème fraîche. Garnish with oregano leaves and season. Toss the lettuce leaves with the extra virgin olive oil and lemon juice, and serve with the bruschetta.

Serves 6

Vegie
Bites

Vegetable samosas

2 tablespoons ghee or oil
1 small onion, diced
1 tablespoon hot curry paste
200 g (7 oz) potatoes, cut into 1 cm
  (1/2 inch) cubes
150 g (5 1/2 oz) orange sweet potato,
  peeled; cut into 1 cm (1/2 inch) cubes
1 tablespoon soft brown sugar
80 g (1/2 cup) frozen peas
50 g (1/3 cup) salted roasted cashew
  nuts, chopped
25 g (1/2 cup) roughly chopped
  coriander (cilantro) leaves
1 kg/2 lb 4 oz (5 sheets) shortcrust
  pastry
oil, for deep-frying

Dipping sauce
500 g (2 cups) thick Greek-style yoghurt
30 g (1 cup) coriander (cilantro)
  leaves, roughly chopped
1 teaspoon ground cumin

Heat the ghee in a large heavy-based saucepan over medium heat. Cook the onion and hot curry paste for 5 minutes, stirring regularly until fragrant and the onion is golden. Add the potato, orange sweet potato and sugar. Cook, stirring regularly, for 8–10 minutes, or until the potatoes are tender. Stir in the peas, reduce the heat to low, cover and cook for a further 5 minutes. If the mixture is sticking, add 1–2 tablespoons of water. Cool to room temperature.

To make the dipping sauce, combine all the ingredients in a bowl and chill until needed.

Season the vegetable mixture then add the cashews and coriander. Using a 7 cm (2 3/4 inch) cutter, cut nine circles from each sheet of pastry. Place 1 rounded teaspoon of filling in the middle of each circle. Fold the pastry over and pinch the sides together.

Fill a deep heavy-based saucepan one-third full of oil and heat to 170°C (325°F), or until a cube of bread browns in 20 seconds. Deep-fry 4 samosas at a time for 3 minutes, or until crisp and the pastry has 'blistered' a little. Drain on paper towels. Serve warm with the dipping sauce.

Makes 45

Ratatouille pies

60 ml (¼ cup) olive oil
1 eggplant (aubergine), diced
1 onion, finely chopped
1 red capsicum (pepper), diced
1 small zucchini (courgette), diced
1 tablespoon tomato paste (purée)
200 g (7 oz) tomatoes, chopped
1 teaspoon dried Italian herbs
750 g (1 lb 10 oz) ready-made
   shortcrust pastry
1 egg, lightly beaten
ready-made pesto, to serve

Heat 2 tablespoons of the oil in a frying pan and cook the eggplant until golden. Remove from the pan. Heat the remaining oil in the pan, add the onion, capsicum and zucchini and cook for 2 minutes. Stir in the tomato paste, fresh tomato, herbs and eggplant. Cook for 20 minutes, or until reduced. Allow to cool.

Meanwhile, preheat the oven to 180°C (350°F/Gas 4) and put a baking tray in the oven. Grease 24 mini muffin holes. Roll the pastry thinly and cut out 24 rounds with a 7 cm (2¾ inch) cutter. Repeat with a 5.5 cm (2¼ inch) cutter. Put one of the larger rounds in each muffin hole and fill with the cooled filling. Dampen the edges of the small rounds and place them on top of the filling to seal the pies. Brush with egg. Put the tin on the hot baking tray and cook for 25 minutes, or until golden. Cool slightly, then remove from the tin. Serve with pesto.

Makes 24

Corn pancakes

6 fresh corn cobs or 325 g (11½ oz)
  can corn kernels, drained
4 spring onions (scallions), finely
  chopped
1 garlic clove, crushed
1 teaspoon curry powder
2 tablespoons self-raising flour
1 teaspoon soy sauce
1 egg
oil, for shallow-frying

If using fresh corn, remove the kernels with a sharp knife. Combine the corn, spring onion, garlic, curry powder, flour, soy sauce and egg, mashing lightly with a potato masher. Cover with plastic wrap and chill for 1 hour.

Heat 4 tablespoons of oil in a frying pan. Drop tablespoons of the corn mixture into the pan — avoid overcrowding. Cook over medium heat for 2–3 minutes, on each side, or until golden brown — turn carefully to prevent the pancakes breaking. Remove from the pan and drain on paper towels. Repeat with the remaining mixture.

Delicious served with sweet chilli sauce, if desired.

Makes 12

Zucchini and haloumi fritters

300 g (10½ oz) zucchini (courgette)
4 spring onions (scallions), thinly
  sliced
200 g (7 oz) haloumi cheese, coarsely
  grated
30 g (¼ cup) plain (all-purpose) flour
2 eggs
1 tablespoon chopped dill, plus
  sprigs, to garnish
60 ml (¼ cup) oil
1 lemon, cut into very thin slices,
  seeds removed
90 g (⅓ cup) thick Greek-style
  yoghurt

Coarsely grate the zucchini and squeeze out as much liquid as possible in your hands or in a clean tea towel. Combine the zucchini with the spring onion, haloumi, flour, eggs and dill. Season well with salt and cracked black pepper.

Heat the oil in a large heavy-based frying pan. Form fritters (using heaped teaspoons of the mixture) and cook in batches for 2 minutes each side, or until golden and firm. Drain on crumpled paper towels.

Cut each slice of lemon into quarters or eighths, depending on the size, to make small triangles.

Top each fritter with ½ teaspoon yoghurt, a piece of lemon and a small sprig of dill.

Makes 45

Note: The fritters are best prepared and cooked as close to the serving time as possible or the haloumi tends to go a little tough.

Spinach and feta triangles

1 kg (2 lb 4 oz) English spinach leaves
60 ml (¼ cup) olive oil
1 onion, chopped
10 spring onions (scallions), sliced
20 g (⅓ cup) chopped parsley
1 tablespoon chopped dill
large pinch of ground nutmeg
35 g (⅓ cup) grated Parmesan
   cheese
150 g (5½ oz) crumbled feta cheese
90 g (3¼ oz) ricotta cheese
4 eggs, lightly beaten
40 g (1½ oz) butter, melted
1 tablespoon olive oil, extra
12 sheets filo pastry

Trim any stems from the spinach. Wash the leaves, roughly chop and place in a large pan with a little water clinging to the leaves. Cover and cook over low heat for 5 minutes, or until the leaves have wilted. Drain well and allow to cool slightly before squeezing to remove the excess water.

Heat the oil in a heavy-based frying pan. Add the onion and cook over low heat for 10 minutes, or until tender and golden. Add the spring onion and cook for a further 3 minutes. Remove from the heat. Stir in the spinach, parsley, dill, nutmeg, Parmesan, feta, ricotta and egg. Season well.

Preheat the oven to 180°C (350°F/ Gas 4). Grease two baking trays. Combine the butter with the extra oil. Work with three sheets of pastry at a time, covering the rest with a damp tea towel. Brush each sheet with butter mixture and lay them on top of each other. Halve lengthways.

Place 4 tablespoons of filling on an angle at the end of each strip. Fold the pastry to enclose the filling and form a triangle. Continue folding the triangle over until you reach the end. Brush with the remaining butter mixture and bake for 20 minutes, or until golden brown.

Makes 8

Lentil patties with cumin skordalia

185 g (1 cup) brown lentils
1 teaspoon cumin seeds
90 g (½ cup) burghul (bulgur wheat)
1 tablespoon olive oil
3 garlic cloves, crushed
4 spring onions (scallions), thinly sliced
1 teaspoon ground coriander
3 tablespoons chopped parsley
3 tablespoons chopped mint
2 eggs, lightly beaten
oil, for deep-frying

Skordalia
500 g (1 lb 2 oz) floury potatoes,
    cut into 2 cm (¾ inch) cubes
3 garlic cloves, crushed
½ teaspoon ground cumin
pinch of ground white pepper
185 ml (¾ cup) olive oil
2 tablespoons white vinegar

Place the lentils in a saucepan, add 625 ml (2½ cups) water and bring to the boil. Reduce the heat to low and cook, covered, for 30 minutes, or until soft. Meanwhile, toast the cumin in a dry frying pan over low heat for 1–2 minutes, or until fragrant. Grind. Remove the lentils from the heat and stir in the burghul. Set aside to cool.

Heat the oil in a frying pan and cook the garlic and spring onion for 1 minute. Add the coriander and cumin and cook for 30 seconds. Add to the lentil mixture with the parsley, mint and egg. Mix well. Chill for 30 minutes.

To make the skordalia, cook the potato in a saucepan of boiling water for 10 minutes, or until very soft. Drain and mash until smooth. Add the garlic, cumin, white pepper and 1 teaspoon salt. Gradually add the oil, mixing with a wooden spoon. Add the vinegar.

Roll tablespoons of the lentil mixture into balls, then flatten slightly. Fill a deep heavy-based saucepan or deep-fryer one-third full of oil and heat to 180°C (350°F), or until a cube of bread browns in 15 seconds. Cook the patties in batches for 1–2 minutes, or until crisp and browned. Drain on paper towels. Serve with the skordalia.

Makes 32

Betel and tofu bites

2 tablespoons sugar
24 betel leaves or large basil leaves
1 tablespoon oil
2 garlic cloves, crushed
1 tablespoon grated fresh ginger
2 small red chillies, seeded and finely
  chopped
200 g (7 oz) fried tofu puffs, shredded
2 fresh kaffir (makrut) lime leaves,
  finely shredded
3 tablespoons lime juice
2 tablespoons shaved palm sugar
  or soft brown sugar
3 tablespoons coriander (cilantro)
  leaves
25 g (¼ cup) desiccated coconut,
  toasted

In a bowl, combine the sugar and
500 ml (2 cups) water. Stir in the
betel leaves, soak for 10 minutes,
then drain.

Heat the oil in a frying pan and
cook the garlic, ginger and chilli
over medium heat for 1 minute.
Add the tofu, lime leaves and the
combined lime juice, palm sugar
and coriander. Stir until the tofu is
heated through.

Put 1 tablespoon of the tofu mixture
onto each betel leaf and lightly
sprinkle with coconut. Roll up the
leaves tightly and serve.

Makes 24

To make the filling, soak the vermicelli in boiling water for 5 minutes. Drain and cut into short lengths. Mix with the remaining filling ingredients.

Working with one wrapper at a time, spoon 1 tablespoon of the filling onto one corner (on the diagonal), brush the edges with water and roll up diagonally, tucking in the edges as you go. Repeat with the remaining filling and wrappers.

Fill a wok or deep heavy-based saucepan one-third full of oil and heat until a cube of bread browns in 15 seconds. Cook in batches for 2–3 minutes, or until golden brown. Drain on paper towels. Serve with sweet chilli sauce.

Makes 40

Mini Thai spring rolls

Filling
80 g (3 oz) dried rice vermicelli
2 garlic cloves, crushed
1 carrot, grated
4 spring onions (scallions), finely
   chopped
1 tablespoon sweet chilli sauce
2 teaspoons grated fresh ginger
2 coriander (cilantro) roots, finely
   chopped
1½ tablespoons lime juice
1 teaspoon shaved palm sugar
2 tablespoons chopped coriander
   (cilantro) leaves
3 teaspoons sesame oil
1 tablespoon kecap manis
40 square (12.5 cm/5 inch)
   spring roll wrappers
oil, for deep-frying
sweet chilli sauce, to serve

Spiced carrot soup sip

80 ml (⅓ cup) olive oil
2 teaspoons honey
3 teaspoons ground cumin
3 teaspoons coriander seeds, lightly
  crushed
2 cinnamon sticks, broken in half
1.5 kg (3 lb 5 oz) carrots, cut into
  even chunks (about 3 cm/1¼ inch)
750 ml (3 cups) chicken stock
100 ml (3½ fl oz) cream
185 g (¾ cup) sour cream
3 tablespoons coriander (cilantro)
  leaves

Preheat the oven to 200°C (400°F/ Gas 6). Combine the oil, honey, cumin, coriander seeds, cinnamon sticks, 1 teaspoon salt and plenty of cracked black pepper in a roasting tin. Add the chunks of carrot and mix well to ensure that all the carrot is coated in the spice mixture.

Roast for 1 hour, or until the carrot is tender, shaking the pan occasionally during cooking. Remove from the oven, discard the cinnamon sticks with tongs and allow the carrot to cool slightly.

Transfer half the carrot chunks, 375 ml (1½ cups) of the stock and 250 ml (1 cup) water to a food processor or blender and blend until smooth. Strain through a fine sieve into a clean saucepan. Repeat with the remaining carrots, stock and another 250 ml (1 cup) water. Bring the soup to a simmer and cook for 10 minutes. Add the cream and season to taste. Pour into shot glasses or espresso cups. Garnish each cup with ¼ teaspoon sour cream and a coriander leaf.

Serves 36 (Makes 1.25 litres/5 cups)

Think ahead: The soup can be refrigerated for 2 days or frozen before the cream is added for up to 8 weeks.

Baked stuffed capsicums

2 red capsicums (peppers)
2 yellow capsicums (peppers)
2 teaspoons olive oil
16 basil leaves
2½ tablespoons capers in vinegar,
    drained, rinsed and chopped
3 tablespoons olive oil, extra
2 garlic cloves, crushed
3 teaspoons aged balsamic vinegar

Preheat the oven to 180°C (350°F/ Gas 4). Cut the capsicums in half lengthways, leaving the stem intact (or if they are very large, cut them into quarters). Scrape out the seeds and any excess pith. Drizzle the bottom of an ovenproof dish with the oil, and add the capsicums, skin-side down.

In each capsicum, place 2 basil leaves, then divide the chopped capers among them. Season well with salt and freshly ground pepper.

In a bowl, combine the extra oil with the garlic and balsamic vinegar, and drizzle evenly over the capsicums. Cover the dish with foil, and cook for 10–15 minutes, or until the capsicums have partially cooked.

Remove the foil, and cook for another 15–20 minutes, or until the capsicums are tender and golden on the edges. Serve warm or at room temperature.

Serves 4

Heat the oil in a frying pan, and cook the spring onion, garlic and ginger for 2–3 minutes, or until soft.

Combine the flour and 1 teaspoon salt in a bowl. Stir in the spring onion mixture and the chopped coriander. Gradually stir in 250 ml (1 cup) boiling water, stopping when a loose dough forms. Knead the dough with floured hands for 1½–2 minutes, or until smooth. Cover with plastic wrap and rest for 30 minutes. Break off walnut-sized pieces of dough and roll them out into thin ovals.

Spring onion flatbreads

2 teaspoons oil
185 g (6½ oz) spring onions (scallions), thinly sliced
1 garlic clove, crushed
½ teaspoon grated fresh ginger
215 g (1¾ cups) plain (all-purpose) flour
1½ tablespoons chopped coriander (cilantro)
oil, for shallow-frying

Fill a large frying pan with 2 cm (¾ inch) oil and heat over medium heat. Cook the breads 2–3 at a time for 25–30 seconds each side, or until crisp and golden. Drain on paper towels and serve warm.

Makes 40

Vegetable shapes with crème fraîche and fried leek

850 g (1 lb 14 oz) long thin
   orange sweet potatoes
5 beetroots
125 g (½ cup) crème fraîche
1 garlic clove, crushed
¼ teaspoon grated lime zest
oil, for deep-frying
2 leeks, cut lengthways into
   very fine slices

Bring two large saucepans of water to the boil over high heat and place the sweet potatoes in one and the beetroots in the other. Boil, covered, for 30–40 minutes, or until tender, adding more boiling water if it starts to evaporate. Drain separately and set aside until cool enough to touch. Remove the skins from the beetroots. Trim the ends from the beetroots and sweet potatoes and cut both into 1 cm (½ inch) slices. Using a biscuit cutter, cut the thin slices into shapes. Leave to drain on paper towels.

Place the crème fraîche, garlic and lime zest in a bowl and mix together well. Refrigerate until ready to use.

Fill a deep heavy-based saucepan one-third full of oil and heat until a cube of bread dropped into the oil browns in 10 seconds. Cook the leek in four batches for 30 seconds, or until golden brown and crisp. Drain well on crumpled paper towels and season with salt.

To assemble, place a teaspoon of the crème fraîche mixture on top of each vegetable shape and top with some fried leek.

Makes 35

Carrots with coconut, ginger and chilli

1 kg (2 lb 4 oz) carrots, peeled
   and cut into thick batons
60 g (2¼ oz) creamed coconut
   (in a block)
1 garlic clove, crushed
2 teaspoons grated fresh ginger
2 green chillies, seeded and
   chopped
1 teaspoon ground coriander
1 teaspoon ground cumin
1 teaspoon soy sauce
1 teaspoon chopped lime zest
1 tablespoon lime juice
1 teaspoon palm sugar
3 tablespoons peanut oil
2 tablespoons chopped coriander
   (cilantro) leaves
lime wedges, to serve

Preheat the oven to 200°C (400°F/
Gas 6). Bring a large saucepan of
water to the boil, blanch the carrots
for 5 minutes, then drain well.

Grate the creamed coconut and mix
with 2–3 tablespoons of hot water to
form a paste. Stir in the garlic, ginger,
chilli, coriander, cumin, soy sauce,
lime zest, lime juice and palm sugar.
Add the carrots and toss to combine.

Pour the peanut oil into a large,
shallow-sided roasting tin and heat
in the oven for 5 minutes. Toss the
carrots in the hot oil, then roast in the
oven for 5 minutes. Reduce the heat
to 180°C (350°F/Gas 4) and roast for
another 20 minutes, or until crisp and
golden. Sprinkle with the coriander
leaves and serve with lime wedges.

Serves 6

Stuffed chillies

1 teaspoon cumin seeds
12 mild small jalapeño or similar mild
  oblong-shaped fat chillies,
  approximately 4 cm x 3 cm
  (1½ inch x 1¼ inch)
1 tablespoon olive oil
2 garlic cloves, finely chopped
½ small red onion, finely chopped
125 g (½ cup) cream cheese,
  softened
30 g (¼ cup) coarsely grated Cheddar
  cheese
2 tablespoons finely chopped drained
  sun-dried tomatoes
1 tablespoon chopped coriander
  (cilantro)
1 teaspoon finely chopped lime zest
pinch of smoked paprika
50 g (½ cup) coarse dry breadcrumbs
2 teaspoons lime juice

Preheat the oven to 200°C (400°F/
Gas 6). Line a baking tray with baking
paper. Toast the cumin seeds in a dry
frying pan for 1–2 minutes, or until
fragrant. Cool slightly, then grind
the seeds.

Cut the chillies lengthways through
the middle. Wearing gloves, remove
the seeds and membranes. Bring a
saucepan of water to the boil, add the
chillies and cook for 1 minute, or until
the water comes back to the boil.
Drain, rinse under cold water, then
return to a saucepan of fresh boiling
water for another minute before
draining, rinsing, then draining again.

Heat the oil in a non-stick frying pan
and cook the garlic and onion over
medium–low heat for 4–5 minutes,
or until the onion softens. Mash the
cream cheese in a bowl, add the
Cheddar, sun-dried tomato, coriander,
lime zest, paprika, cumin and half the
breadcrumbs, and mix well. Stir in the
onion and season. Fill each chilli with
one heaped teaspoon of the mixture,
then lay on the baking tray and scatter
with the remaining breadcrumbs.

Bake for 20 minutes. Squeeze some
lime juice over the top and garnish
with coriander leaves.

Makes 24

Chargrilled eggplant with fresh lemon pesto

2 large eggplants (aubergines),
  cut into 1.5 cm (⅝ inch) slices
  or 8 small eggplants (aubergines),
  halved lengthways
160 ml (⅔ cup) extra virgin olive oil
60 g (2 cups) basil leaves
20 g (1 cup) parsley
50 g (⅓ cup) pine nuts, toasted
1½ garlic cloves
60 g (2¼ oz) grated Parmesan
  cheese
grated zest of 1 lemon
60 ml (¼ cup) lemon juice

Brush both sides of the eggplant slices with 2 tablespoons of extra virgin olive oil. Heat a chargrill pan (griddle) until hot, and cook the eggplant slices for 3 minutes, or until golden and cooked through on both sides. If you are using baby eggplant, grill only on the cut side, and finish off in a 200°C (400°F/Gas 6) oven for 5–8 minutes, or until soft. Cover the eggplant to keep warm.

Place the basil, parsley, pine nuts, garlic, Parmesan, lemon zest and lemon juice in a food processor, and blend together. Slowly add the remaining olive oil and process until the mixture forms a smooth paste. Season with salt and freshly ground black pepper.

Stack the eggplant on a platter, drizzling some pesto between each layer. Serve immediately.

Serves 4–6

Fresh rice paper rolls

Dipping sauce
60 ml (¼ cup) sweet chilli sauce
1 tablespoon lime juice

100 g (3½ oz) dried rice vermicelli
½ green mango, julienned
1 small Lebanese (short) cucumber,
    seeded and julienned
½ avocado, julienned
4 spring onions (scallions), thinly
    sliced
15 g (½ cup) coriander (cilantro)
    leaves
2 tablespoons chopped Vietnamese
    mint
1 tablespoon sweet chilli sauce
2 tablespoons lime juice
20 square (15 cm/6 inch) rice
    paper wrappers

To make the dipping sauce, mix together the chilli sauce and lime juice.

Place the vermicelli in a bowl, cover with boiling water and leave for 5 minutes, or until softened. Drain, then cut into short lengths.

Put the vermicelli, mango, cucumber, avocado, spring onion, coriander, mint, sweet chilli sauce and lime juice in a bowl and mix together well.

Working with no more than two rice paper wrappers at a time, dip each wrapper in a bowl of warm water for 10 seconds to soften, then lay out on a flat work surface. Put 1 tablespoon of the filling on the wrapper, fold in the sides and roll up tightly. Repeat with the remaining filling and rice paper wrappers. Serve immediately with the dipping sauce.

Makes 20

Note: Ensure the rice paper rolls are tightly rolled together or they will fall apart while you are eating them. These rolls can be made 2–3 hours ahead of time — layer the rolls in an airtight container between sheets of greaseproof paper or plastic wrap, then store in the refrigerator.

Indonesian peanut fritters

Dipping sauce
1 tablespoon rice vinegar
1 tablespoon mirin
2 tablespoons kecap manis
¼ teaspoon finely grated
    fresh ginger

175 g (1 cup) rice flour
1 garlic clove, crushed
1 teaspoon ground turmeric
½ teaspoon ground cumin
3 teaspoons sambal oelek
1½ teaspoons ground coriander
1 tablespoon finely chopped
    coriander (cilantro) leaves
200 ml (7 fl oz) coconut milk
200 g (1¼ cups) roasted unsalted
    peanuts
oil, for deep-frying

To make the dipping sauce, combine all the ingredients and cover.

To make the peanut fritters, combine the flour, garlic, turmeric, cumin, sambal oelek, ground coriander, coriander leaves and ½ teaspoon salt in a bowl. Gradually add the coconut milk until the mixture is smooth. Stir in the peanuts and 50 ml (1¾ fl oz) hot water.

Fill a wok or deep heavy-based saucepan one-third full of oil and heat until a cube of bread dropped into the oil browns in 15 seconds. Cook level tablespoons of mixture in batches for 1–2 minutes, or until golden. Drain on paper towels and season well. Serve at once with the dipping sauce.

Makes 25

Cheese and chilli shapes

155 g (1¼ cups) plain (all-purpose)
  flour
pinch dry hot mustard
90 g (3¼ oz) butter, roughly chopped
60 g (½ cup) grated vintage Cheddar
  cheese
4 red chillies, seeded and sliced
1 egg yolk

Process the flour, mustard and butter until they resemble fine breadcrumbs. Add the cheese and chilli, then the egg yolk and 1 tablespoon water, and process until the mixture comes together. Gather into a ball, cover with plastic wrap and refrigerate for 30 minutes.

Preheat the oven to 190°C (375°F/ Gas 5). On a lightly floured surface, roll out the dough to a 5 mm (¼ inch) thickness. Cut into 5 cm (2 inch) rounds.

Place on lightly greased baking trays and bake for 15–20 minutes, or until golden. Cool.

Makes 26

Stuffed zucchini flowers

75 g (2½ oz) plain (all-purpose) flour
100 g (3½ oz) mozzarella cheese
10 basil leaves, torn
20 zucchini (courgette) blossoms,
  stems and pistils removed
olive oil, for shallow-frying
2 lemon wedges, to serve

In a bowl, combine the flour with about 250 ml (1 cup) water, enough to obtain a creamy consistency. Add a pinch of salt and mix.

Cut the mozzarella cheese into 20 matchsticks. Insert a piece of mozzarella and some basil into each zucchini blossom. Gently press the petals closed.

Pour oil into a heavy-based frying pan to a depth of 2.5 cm (1 inch). Heat until a drop of batter sizzles when dropped in the oil.

Dip one flower at a time in the batter, shaking off the excess. Cook in batches for 3 minutes, or until crisp and golden. Drain on paper towels. Season and serve immediately with lemon wedges.

Makes 20

Vegetable frittata with hummus and black olives

2 large red capsicums (peppers)
600 g (1 lb 5 oz) orange sweet
    potato, cut into 1 cm (½ inch)
    slices
60 ml (¼ cup) olive oil
2 leeks, finely sliced
2 garlic cloves, crushed
250 g (9 oz) zucchini (courgettes),
    thinly sliced
500 g (1 lb 2 oz) eggplant
    (aubergines), cut into 1 cm
    (½ inch) slices
8 eggs, lightly beaten
2 tablespoons finely chopped basil
125 g (1¼ cups) grated Parmesan
    cheese
200 g (7 oz) ready-made hummus
black olives, pitted and halved,
    to garnish

Cut the capsicums into large pieces, removing the seeds and membrane. Place, skin-side up, under a hot grill (broiler) until the skin blackens and blisters. Cool in a plastic bag. Peel.

Cook the sweet potato in a saucepan of boiling water for 4–5 minutes, or until just tender. Drain.

Heat 1 tablespoon of the oil in a deep round 23 cm (9 inch) frying pan and stir the leek and garlic over medium heat for 1 minute, or until soft. Add the zucchini and cook for 2 minutes, then remove from the pan.

Heat the remaining oil and cook the eggplant in batches for 2 minutes each side, or until golden. Line the base of the pan with half the eggplant, then the leek. Cover with the capsicum, remaining eggplant and sweet potato.

Combine the eggs, basil, Parmesan and some pepper. Pour the mixture over the vegetables. Cook over low heat for 15 minutes, or until almost cooked. Put the pan under a hot grill (broiler) for 2–3 minutes, or until golden and cooked. Cool, then invert onto a board. Cut into 30 squares. Top with hummus and half an olive.

Makes 30 pieces

Capsicum rolled with goat's cheese, basil and capers

4 large red capsicums (peppers)
5 g (¼ cup) flat-leaf (Italian) parsley, chopped
2 tablespoons chives, chopped
2 tablespoons baby capers, finely chopped
1 tablespoon balsamic vinegar
150 g (5½ oz) goat's cheese
16 basil leaves
olive oil, to cover
crusty Italian bread, to serve

Cut the capsicum into large flat pieces and remove any seeds. Place on a tray skin-side up under a hot grill (broiler) until the skin blisters and blackens. Place in a plastic bag and leave to cool, then peel away the skin. Cut into 3 cm (1¼ inch) wide pieces.

Combine the parsley, chives, capers and balsamic vinegar in a small bowl. Crumble in the goat's cheese, and mix well. Season with lots of pepper. Place a basil leaf on the inside of each capsicum piece, and top with a teaspoon of the goat's cheese mixture. Roll the capsicum over the goat's cheese and secure with a toothpick. Place in an airtight, non-reactive container and cover with olive oil. Refrigerate until required. Allow to return to room temperature before serving with crusty Italian bread.

Serves 4

Seasonal vegetable platter with saffron aïoli

Saffron aïoli
pinch saffron threads
2 egg yolks
3 garlic cloves, crushed
2 tablespoons lemon juice
315 ml (1¼ cups) canola oil

335 g (1 bunch) baby (dutch) carrots,
   scrubbed and trimmed, leaving
   2 cm (¾ inch) green stem
155 g (1 bunch) green asparagus,
   ends trimmed
100 g (3½ oz) baby corn
100 g (3½ oz) French beans, trimmed
2 witlof (chicory/Belgian endive),
   base trimmed and leaves separated
300 g (10½ oz) radishes, trimmed
   and washed well
sea salt and crusty bread, to serve

To make the aïoli, place the saffron in a small bowl with 1 tablespoon of water. Put the egg yolks into a food processor with the garlic and lemon juice and blend until smooth. With the motor running, start adding the canola oil, a few drops at a time until an emulsion forms, then add the remainder in a slow, steady stream until thick and fully combined. Slowly add 2 tablespoons of warm water to thin slightly, and season well with salt and white pepper. Spoon into a small bowl, and stir in the saffron water. Refrigerate until needed.

Blanch the carrots in boiling salted water for 3 minutes, then drain and refresh in cold water. (Or, if you like the crunch, serve them raw.) Blanch the asparagus in boiling salted water for 2 minutes until tender to the bite. Drain and refresh in cold water. Blanch the baby corn in boiling salted water for 1 minute, then drain and refresh. Blanch the French beans for 30 seconds in boiling salted water, drain and refresh.

Arrange all the vegetables on a serving platter with the saffron aïoli. Serve with sea salt and crusty bread.

Serves 4–6

Vegetable pakoras with spiced yoghurt

Spiced yoghurt
1 teaspoon cumin seeds
200 g (7 oz) plain yoghurt
1 garlic clove, crushed
15 g (½ cup) coriander (cilantro)
  leaves, chopped

35 g (⅓ cup) besan (chickpea flour)
40 g (⅓ cup) self-raising flour
45 g (⅓ cup) soy flour
½ teaspoon ground turmeric
1 teaspoon cayenne pepper
½ teaspoon ground coriander
1 small green chilli, seeded and
  finely chopped
oil, for deep-frying
200 g (7 oz) cauliflower, cut into
  small florets
140 g (5 oz) orange sweet potato,
  cut into 5 mm (¼ inch) slices
180 g (6 oz) eggplant (aubergine),
  cut into 5 mm (¼ inch) slices
180 g (6 oz) fresh asparagus, cut
  into 6 cm (2½ inch) lengths

To make the spiced yoghurt, heat a small frying pan over medium heat. Add the cumin seeds and dry-fry for 1–2 minutes, or until aromatic (shake the pan frequently to prevent the seeds from burning). Transfer to a mortar and pestle or spice grinder and roughly grind. Whisk into the yoghurt with the garlic. Season with salt and freshly ground black pepper, then stir in the coriander. Place the besan, self-raising and soy flours, turmeric, cayenne, ground coriander, chilli and 1 teaspoon salt in a bowl. Gradually whisk in 250 ml (1 cup) cold water to form a batter. Leave for 15 minutes. Preheat the oven to 120°C (250°F/Gas ½).

Fill a small saucepan one-third full of oil and heat until a cube of bread browns in 20 seconds. Dip the vegetables in the batter and deep-fry in small batches for 1–2 minutes, or until pale gold. Remove with a slotted spoon and drain well on paper towels. Keep warm in the oven until all the vegetables are cooked.

Serve the hot vegetable pakoras with the spiced yoghurt.

Serves 4

Roasted field mushrooms with tarragon and lemon crème fraîche

80 ml (⅓ cup) olive oil
2 tablespoons lemon juice
4 garlic cloves, crushed
12 large flat field mushrooms,
    brushed and stems trimmed
2 tablespoons finely chopped
    flat-leaf (Italian) parsley
toasted bread, to serve

Lemon crème fraîche
60 ml (¼ cup) crème fraîche
2 teaspoons lemon juice
1 garlic clove, crushed
2 teaspoons chopped tarragon

Preheat the oven to 200°C (400°F/ Gas 6). In a large roasting tin, combine the oil, lemon juice and garlic. Add the mushrooms, and gently toss until coated. Season well with salt and pepper and arrange in a single layer. Roast for 30 minutes, turning to cook evenly.

Meanwhile, in a small bowl, combine the crème fraîche, lemon juice, garlic and tarragon.

Sprinkle the mushrooms and their cooking juices with parsley, and serve with the lemon crème fraîche and toasted bread.

Serves 4

Mini spinach pies

80 ml (⅓ cup) olive oil
2 onions, finely chopped
2 garlic cloves, chopped
150 g (5½ oz) small button
  mushrooms, roughly chopped
200 g (7 oz) English spinach,
  chopped
½ teaspoon chopped thyme
100 g (3½ oz) feta cheese, crumbled
750 g (1 lb 10 oz) home-made or
  bought shortcrust pastry
milk, to glaze

Heat 2 tablespoons of oil in a frying pan over medium heat and cook the onion and garlic for 5 minutes, or until soft and lightly coloured. Add the mushrooms and cook for 4 minutes, or until softened. Transfer to a bowl.

Heat 1 tablespoon of oil in the same pan over medium heat, add half the spinach and cook, stirring well, for 2–3 minutes, or until the spinach has softened. Add to the bowl with the onion. Repeat with the remaining oil and spinach. Add the thyme and feta to the bowl and mix. Season with salt and pepper and set aside to cool.

Preheat the oven to 200°C (400°F/ Gas 6) and grease two 12-hole round-based patty tins. Roll out half the pastry between two sheets of baking paper and cut out 24 rounds using a 7.5 cm (2¾ inch) cutter. Use these to line the patty tins, then divide the spinach mixture among the holes. Roll out the remaining pastry between the baking paper and cut out 24 rounds using a 7 cm (2¾ inch) cutter to top the pies. Cover the pies with the lids and press the edges with a fork to seal. Prick the tops once with a fork, brush with milk and bake for 15–20 minutes, or until golden.

Makes 24

Stuffed artichokes

40 g (¼ cup) raw almonds
4 young globe artichokes
150 g (5½ oz) fresh ricotta cheese
2 garlic cloves, crushed
80 g (1 cup) fresh coarse
  breadcrumbs
1 teaspoon finely grated lemon zest
50 g (½ cup) grated Parmesan
  cheese
7 g (¼ cup) chopped flat-leaf (Italian)
  parsley
1 tablespoon olive oil
2 tablespoons butter
2 tablespoons lemon juice

Preheat the oven to 180°C (350°F/ Gas 4). Spread the almonds on a baking tray and bake for 5–10 minutes, or until lightly golden. Keep a close watch, as the almonds will burn easily. Cool, remove from the tray and chop.

Remove any tough outer leaves from the artichokes. Cut across the artichokes, about 3 cm (1¼ inches) from the top, and trim the stalks, leaving about 2 cm (¾ inch). Rub with lemon and put in a bowl of cold water with a little lemon juice to prevent the artichokes from turning brown.

Combine the almonds, ricotta, garlic, breadcrumbs, lemon zest, Parmesan and parsley in a bowl and season. Gently separate the artichoke leaves and push the filling in between them. Place the artichokes carefully in a steamer and drizzle with the olive oil. Steam for 25–30 minutes, or until tender (test with a metal skewer). Remove and cook under a hot grill (broiler) for about 5 minutes to brown the filling.

Melt the butter in a saucepan, remove from the heat and stir in the lemon juice. Arrange the artichokes on a serving plate, drizzle with the butter sauce and season well.

Serves 4

Tempura vegetables with wasabi mayonnaise

Wasabi mayonnaise
2 tablespoons whole-egg mayonnaise
3 teaspoons wasabi paste
½ teaspoon grated lime zest

2 egg yolks
250 ml (1 cup) chilled soda water
30 g (¼ cup) cornflour (cornstarch)
110 g (4 oz) plain (all-purpose) flour
40 g (¼ cup) sesame seeds, toasted
oil, for deep-frying
1 small (250 g/9 oz) eggplant
  (aubergine), cut into thin rounds
1 large onion, cut into thin rounds,
  with rings intact
300 g (10½ oz) orange sweet potato,
  cut into thin rounds

To make the wasabi mayonnaise, combine all the ingredients. Transfer to a serving bowl, cover with plastic wrap and refrigerate.

Place the egg yolks and soda water in a jug and mix lightly with a whisk. Sift the cornflour and flour into a bowl. Add the sesame seeds and a good sprinkling of salt and mix well. Pour the soda water and egg yolk mixture into the flour and stir lightly with a fork or chopsticks until just combined but still lumpy.

Fill a deep heavy-based saucepan or wok one-third full of oil and heat until a cube of bread dropped into the oil browns in 15 seconds. Dip pairs of the vegetables — eggplant and onion or eggplant and sweet potato — into the batter and cook in batches for 3–4 minutes, or until golden brown and cooked through. Drain on crumpled paper towels; season well. Keep warm, but do not cover or the tempura coating will go soggy.

Transfer the tempura to a warmed serving platter and serve immediately with the wasabi mayonnaise.

Serves 4–6

Spreads
Dips &
Dippers

Guacamole

2 large ripe avocados
2 tablespoons lime juice
1 tomato, seeded and finely diced
1 red chilli, finely chopped
2 tablespoons finely diced red onion
1½ tablespoons chopped coriander
  (cilantro) leaves
1½ tablespoons sour cream
1 tablespoon olive oil
½ teaspoon ground cumin
pinch of cayenne pepper

Put the avocado and lime juice in a large bowl, then mash. Stir in the diced tomato, chilli, onion, coriander, sour cream, olive oil and cumin. Season with cayenne pepper and some salt and pepper.

Spoon into a serving bowl and sprinkle with cayenne pepper.

Makes 2 cups

Pork and peanut dip

Paste
2 small dried red chillies
2 teaspoons chopped coriander
   (cilantro) root
3 teaspoons ground white pepper
6 garlic cloves, chopped
4 red Asian shallots, chopped

1 tablespoon peanut oil
300 g (10½ oz) minced (ground) pork
2 makrut (kaffir) lime leaves
250 ml (1 cup) coconut cream
50 g (⅓ cup) peanuts, toasted and
   chopped
1½ tablespoons lime juice
3 tablespoons fish sauce
2 tablespoons grated palm sugar or
   soft brown sugar
1 tablespoon finely shredded Thai
   basil or coriander (cilantro) leaves
peanut oil, for deep-frying
150 g (5½ oz) cassava crackers

Soak the chillies in boiling water for 15 minutes. Remove the seeds and chop. Blend all of the paste ingredients in a food processor until smooth — add water if necessary.

Heat the oil in a saucepan. Add the paste and cook, stirring frequently, over medium heat, for 15 minutes, or until the paste darkens. Add the pork and stir for 5 minutes, or until coloured. Gradually add the lime leaves and coconut cream, scraping the base of the pan. Cook for 40 minutes, stirring frequently, until the liquid has almost evaporated. Add the peanuts, lime juice, fish sauce and sugar, and cook for 10 minutes, or until the oil begins to separate. Remove from the heat, discard the lime leaves and stir in the basil.

Fill a deep heavy-based saucepan one-third full of oil and heat to 180°C (350°F), or until a cube of bread browns in 15 seconds. Break the crackers in half. Deep-fry in small batches until pale, golden and puffed. Remove immediately and drain. Serve with the dip.

Serves 6–8

White bean dip

2 x 400 g (14 oz) cans lima or
   cannellini beans, drained and rinsed
125 ml (½ cup) olive oil
80 ml (⅓ cup) lemon juice
3 garlic cloves, finely chopped
1 tablespoon finely chopped rosemary

Place the beans in a food processor with the oil, lemon juice, garlic and rosemary and 1 teaspoon salt. Process until smooth, then season with cracked black pepper.

Makes 3 cups

Note: This dip improves with age, so you can make it up to 2 days ahead of time.

Tortilla shards

2 tablespoons sweet paprika
¼ teaspoon cayenne pepper
oil, for deep-frying
8 large flour tortillas, cut into long
   triangles

Combine the paprika and cayenne
pepper in a small bowl.

Fill a deep heavy-based saucepan
one-third full of oil and heat to 180°C
(350°F), or until a cube of bread
dropped into the oil browns in
15 seconds. Drop the tortilla shards
in the oil in batches and deep-fry until
crisp. Drain on crumpled paper towels
and sprinkle lightly with the paprika
mix while still hot.

Serves 8–10

Warm crab and lemon dip

80 g (2¾ oz) butter
2 garlic cloves, crushed
3 French shallots, thinly sliced
1 teaspoon mustard powder
½ teaspoon cayenne pepper
125 ml (½ cup) cream
150 g (5½ oz) cream cheese
60 g (½ cup) grated Cheddar cheese
350 g (12 oz) can crab meat, drained
2 tablespoons lemon juice
2 teaspoons Worcestershire sauce
3 teaspoons chopped tarragon
40 g (½ cup) fresh breadcrumbs
1 tablespoon chopped parsley

Preheat the oven to 170°C (325°F/ Gas 3). Melt half the butter in a saucepan, then cook the garlic and shallots for 2–3 minutes, or until just softened. Add the mustard powder, cayenne pepper and cream. Bring to a simmer and slowly whisk in the cream cheese, a little at a time. When the cream cheese is completely incorporated, whisk in the Cheddar and allow to cook, stirring constantly, over very low heat for 1–2 minutes, or until smooth. Remove from the heat and add the crab meat, lemon juice, Worcestershire sauce and 2 teaspoons of the tarragon. Season to taste with salt and freshly cracked black pepper. Mix, then transfer to a small baking dish.

Melt the remaining butter in a small saucepan, add the breadcrumbs, chopped parsley and remaining tarragon and stir until just combined. Sprinkle over the crab mixture and bake for 15 minutes, or until golden. Serve warm.

Makes 2½ cups

Chorizo and tomato salsa

2 tablespoons olive oil
250 g (9 oz) chorizo sausage, finely
   chopped
4 garlic cloves, finely chopped
4 small celery stalks, finely chopped
2 bay leaves
1 red onion, finely chopped
2 teaspoons sweet paprika
6 ripe tomatoes, peeled, seeded,
   chopped
2 tablespoons tomato paste (purée)
2 x 130 g (4½ oz) cans corn kernels,
   drained
50 g (1¾ cups) coriander (cilantro)
   leaves, roughly chopped
1 tablespoon sugar

Heat the oil in a large frying pan.
Add the sausage, garlic, celery,
bay leaves, onion and paprika.
Cook, stirring, over medium heat
for 10 minutes.

Add the tomato, tomato paste and
corn and cook over high heat for
5 minutes, or until the tomato is
pulpy and the mixture is thick.

Remove the pan from the heat, stir
through the coriander and sugar and
season. Serve hot.

Makes 3 cups

Roast capsicum and eggplant spread

1 large (450 g/1 lb) eggplant
 (aubergine), halved
2 teaspoons olive oil
1 red capsicum (pepper), halved
2 garlic cloves, crushed
15 g (¼ cup) chopped mint
3 teaspoons balsamic vinegar

Preheat the oven to 200°C (400°F/ Gas 6). Brush the cut side of the eggplant with some of the oil. Place cut-side-up on a baking tray. Brush the skin of the capsicum with the remaining oil and place skin-side-up on the baking tray next to the eggplant. Bake the eggplant and capsicum for about 30–35 minutes, or until the flesh is soft.

Place the capsicum in a plastic bag and leave to cool, then peel away the skin. Allow the eggplant to cool.

Scoop the flesh out of the eggplant and place in a food processor with the capsicum, garlic, mint and balsamic vinegar. Season to taste and process until smooth.

Makes 2 cups

Mixed Asian crisps

oil, for deep-frying
16 cassava crackers, broken into
small pieces (see Note)
16 round won ton wrappers
16 small uncooked plain prawn
(shrimp) crackers
1 sheet toasted nori, shredded

Fill a deep heavy-based saucepan or deep-fryer one-third full of oil and heat to 180°C (350°F), or until a cube of bread dropped into the oil browns in 15 seconds.

Deep-fry the cassava pieces until crisp. Remove with a slotted spoon and drain on crumpled paper towels. Repeat with the won ton wrappers and prawn chips.

When they are all cool, combine and toss with the nori.

Makes a large bowl

Note: Cassava crackers are made from the flour of the dried cassava root. Available from Asian food stores.

Herb cheese log

500 g (1 lb 2 oz) cream cheese,
   softened
1 tablespoon lemon juice
1 garlic clove, crushed
2 teaspoons chopped thyme
2 teaspoons chopped tarragon
1 tablespoon chopped flat-leaf
   (Italian) parsley
50 g (1 cup) snipped chives

Put the cream cheese in a large bowl and beat with electric beaters until soft and creamy. Mix in the lemon juice and garlic. In a separate bowl, combine the thyme, tarragon and chopped parsley.

Line a 20 cm x 30 cm (8 inch x 12 inch) tin with foil. Spread the chives over the base of the tin, then spoon the cream cheese mixture over the chives. Using a palette knife, gently spread the mixture into the tin, pushing it into any gaps. Sprinkle the combined herbs evenly over the top.

Lift the foil from the tin and place on a work surface. Roll the cheese into a log, starting from the longest edge, then cover and place on a baking tray. Refrigerate for at least 3 hours, or preferably overnight.

Makes a 30 cm (12 inch) log

Linseed crackers

125 g (1 cup) plain (all-purpose) flour
1/2 teaspoon baking powder
1/2 teaspoon sugar
2 tablespoons linseeds
60 ml (1/4 cup) milk
2 tablespoons olive oil

Preheat the oven to 200°C (400°F/ Gas 6). Process the flour, baking powder, sugar and 1/2 teaspoon salt in a food processor. Add pepper to taste, and stir in the linseeds. Add the milk and oil and mix to form a wet crumbly mixture, adding extra milk if the mixture is too dry.

Turn the mixture out onto a flat, lightly floured surface and bring the mixture together into a ball.

Divide the mixture in half, place one half between two sheets of baking paper and roll out to a thickness of 2–3 mm (1/8 inch). Prick liberally with a fork. Cut the dough into 12 irregular triangles and arrange in a single layer on a lightly greased baking tray. Repeat with the remaining dough.

Bake for 15–20 minutes, or until the bases are lightly golden. Turn over and bake for a further 4–5 minutes, or until the other side is also lightly golden. Transfer to a wire rack to cool completely.

Makes 24

Aïoli with crudités

Aïoli
4 garlic cloves, crushed
2 egg yolks
315 ml (1¼ cups) light olive or
  vegetable oil
1 tablespoon lemon juice
pinch of ground white pepper

12 asparagus spears, trimmed
12 radishes, trimmed
½ telegraph cucumber, seeded,
  halved lengthways and cut
  into batons
1 head of witlof (chicory/Belgian
  endive), leaves separated

For the aïoli, place the garlic, egg yolks and a pinch of salt in a food processor and process for 10 seconds. With the motor running, add the oil in a thin, slow stream. The mixture will start to thicken. When this happens you can add the oil a little faster. Process until all the oil is incorporated and the mixture is thick and creamy. Stir in the lemon juice and white pepper.

Bring a saucepan of water to the boil, add the asparagus and cook for 1 minute. Remove and plunge into a bowl of iced water.

Arrange the asparagus, radish, cucumber and witlof decoratively on a platter and place the aïoli in a bowl on the platter. The aïoli can also be used as a sandwich spread or as a sauce for chicken or fish.

Serves 4

Note: It is important that all the ingredients are at room temperature when making this recipe. Should the aïoli start to curdle, beat in 1–2 teaspoons boiling water. If this fails, put another egg yolk in a clean bowl and very slowly whisk the curdled mixture into it, one drop at a time, then continue as above.

Prawn pâté with garlic toasts

315 ml (1¼ cups) chicken stock
1 tablespoon gelatine
375 g (13 oz) cream cheese, at
  room temperature
800 g (1 lb 12 oz) cooked prawns
  (shrimp), peeled, deveined and
  roughly chopped
2 garlic cloves, crushed
2 tablespoons finely chopped chives
1 tablespoon chopped dill
30 g (1 oz) butter, melted
2 tablespoons olive oil
1 baguette, cut into 7 mm (¼ inch)
  slices

Bring a shallow saucepan of water to the boil. Pour the stock into a heatproof bowl, then sprinkle the gelatine evenly over it; do not stir. Remove the saucepan from the heat and place the bowl of chicken stock in the pan. Stir the gelatine into the stock until it has dissolved; remove the bowl and cool for 30 minutes.

Place the gelatine liquid in a blender, add the cream cheese, half the prawn meat and half of the garlic and blend until smooth. Transfer to a bowl and leave for 20 minutes, or until thickened slightly.

Add the remaining prawn meat, chives and dill and season to taste. Pour into eight 125 ml (½ cup) ramekins. Cover with plastic wrap and refrigerate for 2 hours, or until set.

Preheat the oven to 180°C (350°F/ Gas 4). Combine the butter, oil and remaining garlic and lightly brush both sides of the bread slices with the mixture. Place apart on baking trays and bake for 10 minutes, or until golden and crisp. Leave to cool.

Unmould the pâté and serve with the garlic toasts.

Serves 8

Beetroot hummus

500 g (1 lb 2 oz) beetroot
80 ml (⅓ cup) olive oil
1 large onion, chopped
1 tablespoon ground cumin
400 g (14 oz) tin chickpeas,
    drained
1 tablespoon tahini
80 g (⅓ cup) plain yoghurt
3 garlic cloves, crushed
60 ml (¼ cup) lemon juice
125 ml (½ cup) vegetable stock
Lebanese or Turkish bread, to serve

Scrub the beetroot well. Bring a large saucepan of water to the boil over high heat and cook the beetroot for 35–40 minutes, or until soft and cooked through. Drain and cool slightly before peeling.

Meanwhile, heat 1 tablespoon of the oil in a frying pan over medium heat and cook the onion for 2–3 minutes, or until soft. Add the cumin and cook for a further 1 minute, or until fragrant.

Chop the beetroot and place in a food processor or blender with the onion mixture, chickpeas, tahini, yoghurt, garlic, lemon juice and stock, and process until smooth. With the motor running, add the remaining oil in a thin steady stream. Process until the mixture is thoroughly combined. Serve the hummus with Lebanese or Turkish bread.

Serves 8

Note: You can use 500 g (1 lb 2 oz) of any vegetable to make the hummus. Try carrot or pumpkin.

Spiced soy crackers

155 g (1¼ cups) plain (all-purpose)
  flour
70 g (2½ oz) soy flour
½ teaspoon garam masala
½ teaspoon paprika
2½ tablespoons olive oil
2½ tablespoons lemon juice

Place the flours, garam masala,
paprika and ½ teaspoon salt in a
food processor. Add the oil, lemon
juice and 100 ml (3½ fl oz) water
and blend until the mixture comes
together in a ball. Cover in plastic
wrap and place in the refrigerator
for 1 hour.

Preheat the oven to 160°C (315°F/
Gas 2–3). Line three baking trays with
baking paper. Cut the dough into
5 or 6 pieces, then roll each piece
into rectangles as thinly as possible
— about 2 mm (⅛ inch) thick. Cut
each piece into long thin triangles
(4 cm x 10 cm/1½ inches x 4 inches).
Place on the prepared trays.

Bake for 20 minutes, or until crisp
and lightly coloured. Serve with your
favourite dip.

Makes 24

Taramasalata

5 slices of white bread, crusts
  removed
80 ml (⅓ cup) milk
100 g (3½ oz) tarama (grey mullet roe)
1 egg yolk
½ small onion, grated
1 garlic clove, crushed
2 tablespoons lemon juice
80 ml (⅓ cup) olive oil
bread, for serving

Fish substitution
  smoked cod's roe

Soak the bread in the milk for
10 minutes. Press in a strainer to
extract any excess milk, then mix the
bread in a food processor with the
tarama, egg yolk, onion and garlic for
30 seconds, or until smooth. Mix in
1 tablespoon of the lemon juice.

With the motor running, slowly pour
in the olive oil until the mixture is
smooth. Add the remaining lemon
juice and a pinch of white pepper. If
the dip tastes too salty, add another
piece of bread and blend it together.
Serve the dip with bread.

Makes 1½ cups

Potato, olive oil and garlic dip

460 g (2 cups) mashed potato
3 garlic cloves, crushed
185 ml (³/₄ cup) olive oil
2 tablespoons white wine vinegar
5 tablespoons milk
30 g (¹/₂ cup) chopped herbs

Combine the potato and garlic in a bowl. Using electric beaters, gradually beat in half the oil, then the vinegar, then the remaining oil.

Slowly beat in the milk. Add the herbs and season to taste with salt and freshly ground black pepper.

Makes 2¹/₂ cups

Cheese fruit log

35 g (¼ cup) shelled pistachio nuts
250 g (9 oz) cream cheese, softened
50 g (¼ cup) finely chopped dried
apricots
3 spring onions (scallions), finely
chopped
45 g (¼ cup) sun-dried tomatoes,
drained, finely chopped
10 g (⅓ cup) finely chopped flat-leaf
(Italian) parsley

Preheat the oven to 200°C (400°F/
Gas 6). Place the pistachio nuts
on a lined baking tray and roast
for 5 minutes, or until golden brown.
Cool and finely chop.

Beat the cream cheese until smooth.
Fold in the apricot, onion and sun-
dried tomato, and pepper to taste.

Form the mixture into a 20 cm (8 inch)
log. Roll the log in the combined
pistachio nuts and parsley. Wrap in
plastic wrap and refrigerate until firm.

Makes a 20 cm (8 inch) log

Mushroom pâté with melba toast

50 g (1³⁄₄ oz) butter
1 small onion, chopped
3 garlic cloves, crushed
375 g (13 oz) button mushrooms,
    quartered
125 g (1 cup) slivered almonds,
    toasted
2 tablespoons cream
2 tablespoons finely chopped
    thyme
3 tablespoons finely chopped
    flat-leaf (Italian) parsley
6 thick slices wholegrain or
    wholemeal bread

Heat the butter in a large frying pan. Cook the onion and garlic over medium heat for 2 minutes, or until soft. Increase the heat, add the mushrooms and cook for 5 minutes, or until the mushrooms are soft and most of the liquid has evaporated. Leave to cool for 10 minutes.

Place the almonds in a food processor or blender and chop roughly. Add the mushroom mixture and process until smooth. With the motor running, gradually pour in the cream. Stir in the herbs and season with salt and cracked black pepper. Spoon into two 250 ml (1 cup) ramekins and smooth the surface. Cover and refrigerate for 4–5 hours to allow the flavours to develop.

To make the toast, preheat the oven to 180°C (350°F/Gas 4). Toast one side of the bread under a hot grill (broiler) until golden. Remove the crusts and cut each slice into four triangles. Place on a large oven tray in a single layer, toasted-side down, and cook for 5–10 minutes, or until crisp. Remove as they crisp. Spread with pâté and serve immediately.

Makes 24

Herbed lavash

125 ml (½ cup) olive oil
3 garlic cloves, crushed
6 slices lavash bread
2 teaspoons sea salt flakes
2 teaspoons dried mixed Italian herbs

Preheat the oven to 180°C (350°F/ Gas 4).

Heat the oil and garlic in a small saucepan over low heat until the oil is warm and the garlic is fragrant but not browned.

Brush the lavash bread on both sides with the garlic oil. Cut each piece of bread into eight triangular wedges and position side-by-side on baking trays. Sprinkle the upper side with the sea salt and herbs. Bake the lavash for 8–10 minutes, or until crisp.

Makes about 48 pieces

Tzatziki

2 Lebanese (short) cucumbers
400 g (14 oz) Greek-style plain
  yoghurt
4 garlic cloves, crushed
3 tablespoons finely chopped mint,
  plus extra to garnish
1 tablespoon lemon juice

Cut the cucumbers in half lengthways, scoop out the seeds and discard. Leave the skin on and coarsely grate the cucumber into a small colander. Sprinkle with salt and leave over a large bowl for 15 minutes to drain off any bitter juices.

Meanwhile, place the yoghurt, crushed garlic, mint and lemon juice in a bowl, and stir until well combined.

Rinse the cucumber under cold water then, taking small handfuls, squeeze out any excess moisture. Combine the grated cucumber with the yoghurt mixture then season to taste with salt and freshly ground black pepper. Serve immediately or refrigerate until ready to serve, garnished with the extra mint.

Makes 2 cups

Notes: Tzatziki is often served as a dip with flatbread or Turkish pide but is also suitable to serve as a sauce to accompany seafood and meat. Tzatziki will keep in an airtight container in the refrigerator for 2–3 days.

Red capsicum and walnut dip with toasted pitta wedges

4 large red capsicums (peppers)
1 small red chilli
4 garlic cloves, in the skin
100 g (1 cup) walnuts, lightly
  toasted
50 g (1¾ oz) sourdough bread,
  crusts removed
2 tablespoons lemon juice
1 tablespoon pomegranate
  molasses
1 teaspoon ground cumin
pitta bread
olive oil
sea salt

Cut the capsicum into large flat pieces. Place on a tray skin-side up with the chilli and the whole garlic cloves, and cook under a hot grill (broiler) until the skin blackens and blisters. Transfer to a plastic bag and allow to cool. Gently peel away the capsicum and chilli skin, and remove the garlic skins.

Place the walnuts in a food processor and grind. Add the capsicum and chilli flesh, garlic, bread, lemon juice, pomegranate molasses and cumin, and blend until smooth. Stir in 2 tablespoons of warm water to even out the texture, and season well with salt. Cover and refrigerate overnight so the flavours develop.

Preheat the oven to 200°C (400°F/ Gas 6). Cut the pitta bread into wedges, brush with olive oil and lightly sprinkle with sea salt. Cook in the oven for about 5 minutes, or until golden brown. Allow to cool and become crisp.

Drizzle olive oil over the dip. Serve with the toasted pitta wedges.

Serves 6–8

Spinach pâté

400 g (14 oz) English spinach leaves
30 g (1 oz) butter
½ teaspoon ground coriander
pinch cayenne pepper
2 spring onions (scallions), roughly
   chopped
1 garlic clove
50 g (⅓ cup) blanched almonds
2 teaspoons white wine vinegar
125 g (½ cup) sour cream

Remove the stems from the spinach.
Wash the leaves and place wet in a
pan. Cover and cook for 2 minutes,
or until wilted, then drain, reserving
60 ml (¼ cup) of the cooking liquid.
Cool the spinach, then squeeze dry.

Melt the butter in a small pan. Add
the coriander, cayenne pepper, spring
onion, garlic and almonds, and cook
until the onion is tender. Cool.

Place in a food processor and
process until finely chopped. Add
the spinach and process, gradually
adding the reserved cooking liquid
and vinegar.

Stir in the sour cream and season well
with salt and pepper.

Makes 1½ cups

Place the Kalamata olives, crushed garlic, anchovies, capers, chopped thyme, Dijon mustard, lemon juice, oil and brandy in a food processor and process until smooth. Season to taste with salt and freshly ground black pepper. Spoon into a clean, warm jar, cover with a layer of olive oil, seal and refrigerate for up to 1 week. Serve on bruschetta or with a meze plate.

Makes 1½ cups

Note: To make sure your storage jar is very clean, preheat the oven to 120°C (230°F/Gas ½). Wash the jar and lid thoroughly in hot soapy water (or preferably in a dishwasher) and rinse well with hot water. Put the jar on a baking tray and place in the oven for 20 minutes, or until fully dry and you are ready to use it. Do not dry the jar or lid with a tea towel.

Tapenade

400 g (2²/₃ cups) pitted Kalamata olives
2 garlic cloves, crushed
2 anchovy fillets in oil, drained
2 tablespoons capers in brine, rinsed and squeezed dry
2 teaspoons chopped thyme leaves
2 teaspoons Dijon mustard
1 tablespoon lemon juice
60 ml (¼ cup) olive oil
1 tablespoon brandy, optional

Cocktails

Frozen Splice

15 ml melon liqueur
15 ml white rum
15 ml Malibu
15 ml coconut cream
30 ml pineapple juice
1 cup crushed ice
pineapple wedge, to garnish
pineapple leaves, to garnish

Pour the melon liqueur, white rum, Malibu, coconut cream and pineapple juice into a blender. Add the crushed ice and blend until smooth. Pour into a large, chilled martini glass. Garnish with a wedge of pineapple and pineapple leaves.

Citrus blush

ice cubes
15 ml lime juice
15 ml Limoncello
45 ml gin
cranberry juice, to top up
lime wedge, to garnish

Half-fill an old-fashioned glass with ice. Pour in the lime juice, Limoncello and gin. Stir well to combine, top up with cranberry juice, and garnish with a lime wedge.

Fluffy duck

ice cubes
30 ml advocaat
30 ml gin
15 ml Cointreau
30 ml orange juice
30 ml cream
lemonade, to top up

Half-fill a cocktail glass with ice.
Pour in the advocaat, gin, Cointreau,
orange juice and cream, and top up
with lemonade.

Continental

2 teaspoons lime juice
½ teaspoon sugar
45 ml white rum
crushed ice
15 ml green crème de menthe

Mix the lime juice with the sugar and white rum in an old-fashioned glass, stirring until the sugar dissolves. Half-fill the glass with crushed ice and pour in the crème de menthe. Stir gently to combine.

B52

15 ml Kahlua
15 ml Irish cream
15 ml Cointreau

Pour the Kahlua into a shot glass, then carefully add the Irish cream over the back of a teaspoon to layer. Using a clean teaspoon, layer the Cointreau over the Irish cream.

Watermelon and vodka granita

1 kg piece of watermelon, rind
   removed to give 600 g flesh
2 teaspoons lime juice
¼ cup (60 g) caster sugar
¼ cup (60 ml) citrus-flavoured vodka

Coarsely chop the watermelon, removing the seeds. Place the flesh in a food processor and add the lime juice and sugar. Process until smooth, then strain through a fine sieve. Stir in the vodka, then taste — if the watermelon is not very sweet, you may have to add a little more sugar.

Pour into a shallow 1.5 litre metal tin and freeze for about 1 hour, or until beginning to freeze around the edges. Scrape the frozen parts back into the mixture with a fork. Repeat every 30 minutes for about 4 hours, or until even ice crystals have formed.

Serve immediately or beat with a fork just before serving. To serve, scrape into dishes with a fork.

Serves 4–6

Serving suggestion: A scoop of the granita in a shot glass with vodka is a hit at summer cocktail parties.
Variation: A tablespoon of finely chopped mint may be stirred through the mixture after straining the liquid.

Cherry bombe

ice cubes
30 ml gin
15 ml cherry brandy
15 ml lime juice
15 ml Cointreau
1 teaspoon grenadine
dash bitters
pineapple juice, to top up
pineapple wedge, to garnish
pineapple leaves, to garnish

Half-fill a cocktail shaker with ice.
Pour in the gin, cherry brandy,
lime juice, Cointreau, grenadine
and bitters. Shake well and strain
into a highball glass, half-filled with
ice. Top up with pineapple juice
and garnish with a pineapple wedge
and leaves.

Amaretto sour

ice cubes
30 ml amaretto
30 ml lemon juice
30 ml orange juice
stemmed cherry, to garnish

Half-fill a cocktail shaker with ice. Pour in the amaretto, lemon juice and orange juice and shake well. Strain into a sour glass (similar to a flute glass, but with a short stem). Garnish with the cherry.

Bloody Mary

3 ice cubes
45 ml vodka
4 drops Tabasco
1 teaspoon Worcestershire sauce
10 ml lemon juice
pinch salt
1 grind black pepper
70 ml chilled tomato juice
1 celery stick

Place ice cubes in a highball glass, pour in the vodka, then add the Tabasco, Worcestershire sauce and lemon juice. Add the salt and pepper, then pour in the tomato juice, and stir well. Allow to sit for a minute and garnish with a crisp, fresh stalk of celery.

Illusion

ice cubes
30 ml melon liqueur
30 ml Cointreau
30 ml vodka
30 ml lemon juice
30 ml pineapple juice
pineapple leaves, to garnish

Half-fill a cocktail shaker with ice. Pour in the melon liqueur, Cointreau, vodka, lemon juice and pineapple juice. Shake well, and strain into a large, chilled cocktail glass. Garnish with pineapple leaves.

Havana

ice cubes
60 ml pineapple juice
10 ml cherry brandy
45 ml white rum
stemmed cocktail cherry, to garnish

Half-fill a cocktail shaker with ice.
Pour in the pineapple juice, cherry
brandy and white rum. Shake well,
and strain into a cocktail glass half-
filled with ice. Garnish with a cherry.

Full Moon

ice cubes
30 ml white rum
30 ml Kahlua
1 teaspoon sugar
pinch ground cloves
pinch ground cinnamon
150 ml cold espresso coffee
30 ml cream

Three-quarters fill a highball glass with ice, pour in the rum and Kahlua, and add the sugar. Stir well until the sugar has dissolved, then add the cloves and cinnamon, and top up with cold espresso coffee. Float the cream over the top, by carefully pouring it over the back of a teaspoon.

Black Russian

ice cubes
45 ml vodka
15 ml Kahlua

Place the ice in an old-fashioned glass, add the vodka and Kahlua, and stir.

Lime Rickey

ice cubes
45 ml gin
15 ml sugar syrup
20 ml lime juice
soda water, to top up
lime twist, to garnish
lime slice, to garnish

Half-fill a highball glass with ice. Add the gin, sugar syrup and lime juice, then top up with soda water. Garnish with a twist of lime and a slice of lime.

Hara kiri

ice cubes
30 ml melon liqueur
30 ml white rum
30 ml lemon juice

Half-fill an old-fashioned glass with ice. Add the melon liqueur, white rum and lemon juice. Stir to combine.

The Lost Cherry

30 ml Malibu
30 ml strawberry liqueur
30 ml chocolate liqueur
15 ml cream
1/2 chocolate-coated cherry bar
1 cup crushed ice
chocolate-dipped stemmed cocktail
    cherries or fresh cherries, to garnish

Pour the Malibu, strawberry liqueur, chocolate liqueur and cream into a blender, add the chocolate-coated cherry bar and blend until smooth. Add the crushed ice and blend until the mixture is the consistency of shaved ice. Pour into a large, chilled cocktail glass and garnish with chocolate-dipped cocktail or fresh cherries on skewers.

Long Island iced tea

ice cubes
15 ml white rum
15 ml vodka
15 ml gin
15 ml Cointreau
15 ml tequila
½ teaspoon lime juice
cola, to top up
lime wedge, to garnish

Half-fill a highball glass with ice cubes. Pour in the white rum, vodka, gin, Cointreau, tequila and lime juice, then top up with cola. Stir well with a swizzle stick to combine. Garnish with a wedge of lime.

Blackberry spritzer

ice cubes
30 ml Grand Marnier
15 ml crème de cassis
10 ml lemon juice
6 blackberries
soda water, to top up

Half-fill a highball glass with ice,
and pour in the Grand Marnier,
crème de cassis and lemon juice.
Add the blackberries and top up
with soda water.

Envy

ice cubes
30 ml white rum
15 ml amaretto
15 ml blue Curaçao
15 ml lime juice
75 ml pineapple juice
pineapple wedge, to garnish

Half-fill a cocktail shaker with ice. Pour in the rum, amaretto, blue Curaçao, lime juice and pineapple juice. Shake well then strain into a highball glass, half-filled with ice. Garnish with a wedge of pineapple.

Gin sling

ice cubes
45 ml gin
30 ml lemon juice
dash grenadine
10 ml sugar syrup
soda water, to top up

Half-fill an old-fashioned glass with ice. Add the gin, lemon juice, grenadine and sugar syrup, then top up with soda water. Garnish with a cocktail umbrella.

Japanese slipper

ice cubes
30 ml melon liqueur
30 ml Cointreau
15 ml lemon juice
strips of lemon rind, to garnish

Half-fill a cocktail shaker with
ice. Pour in the melon liqueur,
Cointreau and lemon juice. Shake
well and strain into a chilled martini
glass. Garnish with lemon rind.

Cow's revenge

ice cubes
30 ml creamy chocolate liqueur
15 ml Frangelico
15 ml Irish cream
15 ml butterscotch schnapps
30 ml cream
1 teaspoon chocolate syrup

Half-fill a cocktail shaker with ice. Pour in the chocolate liqueur, Frangelico, Irish cream, butterscotch schnapps, cream and chocolate syrup. Shake well to combine, and strain into a large, chilled cocktail glass.

Bahama mama

ice cubes
15 ml Malibu
15 ml dark rum
15 ml Kahlua
15 ml white rum
crushed ice
pineapple juice, to top up
thin pineapple wedge, to garnish
mint sprig, to garnish

Half-fill a cocktail shaker with ice. Pour in the Malibu, dark rum, Kahlua and white rum. Shake well to mix, then strain into a highball glass half-filled with crushed ice. Top up with pineapple juice. Garnish with a thin pineapple wedge and a small sprig of mint on the rim.

Bourbon sour

ice cubes
80 ml lemon juice
1 ½ teaspoons sugar syrup
60 ml bourbon
soda water, to top up
stemmed cocktail cherry, to garnish
slice of orange, to garnish

Half-fill a cocktail shaker with ice.
Pour in the lemon juice, sugar syrup
and bourbon, shake well and strain
into a highball glass half-filled with ice.
Top up with soda water and garnish
with the cherry and a slice
of orange.

Woo woo

ice cubes
lime wedge
60 ml vodka
15 ml peach schnapps
cranberry juice, to top up

Half-fill a cocktail shaker with ice. Squeeze the lime wedge into the shaker, and add the vodka and peach schnapps. Shake, then strain into an old-fashioned glass half-filled with ice. Add the squeezed lime wedge and top up with cranberry juice.

Fuzzy navel

ice cubes
45 ml peach schnapps
fresh orange juice, to top up

Three-quarters fill a highball glass with ice. Pour in the peach schnapps and top up with fresh orange juice. Garnish with a cocktail umbrella and a swizzle stick.

Index

First published in 2006 by Bay Books, an imprint of Murdoch Books Pty Limited

National Library of Australia Cataloguing-in-Publication Data: is available for this title.

ISBN 1-74045-703-X

Printed by Sing Cheong Printing Company Ltd
PRINTED IN CHINA

IMPORTANT: Those who might be at risk from the effects of salmonella poisoning (the elderly,
pregnant women, young children and those suffering from immune deficiency diseases) should
consult their doctor with any concerns about eating raw eggs.

CONVERSION GUIDE: You may find cooking times vary depending on the oven you are using.
For convection ovens, as a general rule, set the oven temperature to 70¡F lower than indicated
in the recipe.